W9-CNW-905

"Relationships are the foundation of every great school and organization. They are not everything, but without them, you can do nothing. In her new book, Tara Martin reminds us through authentic stories why relationships are so crucial to learning and provides practical suggestions to build on those relationships within your school, even when it seems hard to do."

—**George Couros**, author of *The Innovator's Mindset*

"Writing from the heart and from personal experience, Tara shows you that you have the ability to be more for your students. Don't just say they have potential, show them how they have that potential. Connect with colleagues and peers in meaningful ways and those interactions will turn out positive and only enhance your career and the climate of your classroom. I'm confident you'll love *Be REAL* just as much as I did!"

—**Adam Welcome**, educator, speaker, author, runner

"*Be REAL* is a book that I wish I'd had from my first day in the classroom. Tara Martin does a brilliant job showing us how to educate from the heart. Page after page, I was drawn in by her powerful stories and practical strategies. This book is a true life changer and one that I know I will always hold close as I continue to grow as a leader. Thank you, Tara, for showing us that when we can be anything, we should always be REAL."

—**Beth Houf**, proud principal and coauthor of *Lead Like a PIRATE*

"Every student craves to be loved. Tara Martin gets REAL with us as she shares heartwarming stories of teachers who impacted her soul for a lifetime. Tara shares life-changing tips to ensure you not only light up the heart of a child but become the teacher you set out to be!"

—**LaVonna Roth**, creator and founder of Ignite Your S.H.I.N.E.®

"*Be REAL* is a captivating read that drew me in from the very first page. Tara's REALness is beautiful, raw, heartwarming, and powerful. You will come away inspired, energized, empowered, and with a plethora of practical ideas and strategies that you can use immediately to put the REAL you into your educational world. This book is sure to make a life changing impact on those you serve! Administrators, coaches, and educators everywhere, this book is for you!"

—**Tisha Richmond,** culinary teacher and discovery school lead learner

"This book is like a coffee shop heart-to-heart meet-up with the mentor teacher we've always wanted. Tara Martin fills *Be REAL* with stories that are intricately, beautifully told and provide perspective and wisdom. They'll make you say, 'Oh, I can use that line,' or, 'Oh, now I see how I can respond to that better.' She'll prove to you that just as the human heart can't be replicated, neither can a REAL educator."

—**Matt Miller,** educator, speaker and author of *Ditch That Textbook*

"Tara Martin lives the REAL mantra to her core, and this book beautifully captures her spirit and energy. It is full of authentic stories that highlight what it means to be REAL. You will love this heartfelt manifesto that shows the power of relationships in education. Tara inspires you to connect with those you serve and provides practical strategies to dive in!"

—**Katie Martin,** educator and author of *Learner-Centered Innovation*

"Tara pulls us in and shares with us her unique journey and her deep passion for students, for families and for educators. Woven within her touching stories Tara reminds and empowers us to connect with who we are and who we want to be for students. *Be REAL* is written for anyone ready to take that next step to teach and live from the heart."

—**Carrie Baughcum,** doodler, special education teacher, creator of CarrieBaughcum.com

"Tara Martin's words jump off the page as the heartbeat of education resonates throughout this book. Her compelling stories remind you that you're never alone in seeking out the best for students and staff. She keeps learning at the forefront with thought-provoking questions and a multitude of resources to explore. If you are searching for REAL talk about making a positive impact on yourself and others, then *Be REAL: Educate from the Heart* is the book for you!"

—**Tamara Letter**, technology integrator and instructional coach

"With *Be REAL*, Tara Martin addresses a significant concern for the state of education in the digital age as she calls readers to hold fast to their humanity through an intentional commitment to investing in others. The beauty of this book lies in Tara's ability to lead by example as she shares her personal triumphs, failures, and life lessons, conveying a candid vulnerability that assures readers she does, in fact, practice what she preaches. That authenticity combined with the depth and breadth of her attention to the details of living and leading in this way make *Be REAL* a text with the power to influence any and all practitioners in education."

—**Andrew Easton**, personalized learning coordinator
for Omaha Westside Community Schools

"Tara Martin shares her heart and her soul in *Be REAL*. In this book, Tara shares her experiences and her knowledge of brain science to connect the REAL aspects of education and demonstrate the importance of making deep connections with students and colleagues. From this book, you will take away tools that will help you have an even bigger impact on your school, and more importantly, find a deeper understanding of yourself. Take the time cannonball into *Be REAL*. You won't regret it!"

—**Jay Billy**, elementary principal and author of *Lead With Culture*

Be REAL

Educate from the Heart

Tara Martin

Be REAL

© 2018 by Tara M. Martin

This book is available at special discounts when purchased in quantity for use as premiums, promotions, fundraisers, or for educational use. For inquiries and details, contact the publisher at books@daveburgessconsulting.com.

Published by Dave Burgess Consulting, Inc.
San Diego, CA
DaveBurgessConsulting.com

Cover Design by Genesis Kohler
Editing and Interior Design by My Writers' Connection

Library of Congress Control Number: 2018944897
Paperback ISBN: 978-1-946444-90-5
Ebook ISBN: 978-1-946444-89-9

First Printing: June 2018

This book is dedicated to the one who stole my heart the moment he was born—my incredibly talented son, Kaleb Martin.

Kaleb, no matter what life tosses your way, Be REAL. It is enough.

Contents

Foreword
by Dave Burgess

This book almost didn't happen.

With the due date for the manuscript rapidly approaching, Tara messaged me and said, "I'm out." She was going to pull the plug on her dream of telling her story, influencing educators across the globe, and fulfilling a bucket-list item of epic proportions. Worse yet, the book was basically done.

Fear is a formidable dragon. When that beast rears its ugly head and breathes the fires of doubt, trepidation, and timidity, instinct tells us to cower and run rather than stand and fight. Who doesn't fear the risk of vulnerability? Who wouldn't dread baring one's soul and exposing the rough and rocky reality of the road that led to the dragon's cave?

Nobody would have blamed Tara if she had quit. After all, most people do.

The chances I was going to let that happen ranged approximately between zero and none. I texted back, "You are writing the book, we are publishing it, and we are sending this message out into the world. Finish it."

I wasn't being insensitive; it was just that I knew Tara. She isn't like "most people." She is a fighter. She is a survivor who has scrapped and scratched her way to overcome all odds, defy doubters, and negate the nefarious naysayers who have stood in her path. As she puts it, she "cannonballs in"—risk and rejection be hanged! So with her uncommon courage, Tara slayed the dragon of fear and finished the book. And now we are honored to share it with all of you.

I vividly remember slaying a similar dragon myself. After writing *Teach Like a PIRATE*, I had to decide whether to sign with a big publisher or, with no experience whatsoever, start a publishing company and do it myself. I can still hear the well-intentioned advice many offered at the time:

> *"You'll never get it in a bookstore if you self-publish it."*
>
> *"Nobody will take your book seriously with that cheesy title."*
>
> *"Our marketing department says it won't fit in with other books in the genre."*
>
> *"It's way too personal. You wrote about walking through the canyons with your kids in this book. You wrote about your favorite Christmas carol! That doesn't belong in a professional book."*
>
> *"Where are the footnotes and research? Where is the data to support all of this?"*
>
> *"We suggest removing some of the edgy stuff if you ever hope for administrators to support it."*

Quite simply, the book "they" told me to write was not the book *I* wanted to write. I wanted to share the *real* me and my manifesto about transforming education. I wasn't going to let that story be watered down.

To bring my authentic story to life, Shelley and I had to start our own company. We formed Dave Burgess Consulting, Inc. and published *Teach Like a PIRATE* from a laptop at our kitchen table. Now we have turned our focus to helping others amplify their impact by sharing their authentic stories and building a family of educators who want to change the world and not have their voices stifled or messages stunted by corporate cowardice and conformity.

Tara's message is a perfect example of this rallying cry for authenticity. In this era of fake news, false prophets, and phony Facebook friends, her manifesto is about embracing what truly connects us all—our heart. Sharing our REAL selves can transform education. Nobody changes the world by hiding. You can't play small and expect to do big things. Mediocrity doesn't motivate. Each of us has a tremendous and unique gift to offer the world, and when we allow anything to stand in the way of sharing our gifts—our *real* selves—we cheat the universe.

In *Be REAL: Educate from the Heart*, Tara freely shares her gift, inspires us to share ours, and shows the path to do it. You have no more excuses for not making a splash. Be real.

There Are Some Things Technology Can't Replace

We live in a world where technology seems to be taking over. Machines and artificial intelligence (AI) have changed the way we work—and have even replaced employees in some jobs and industries. We have cars that drive themselves, drones that deliver products, and grocery stores that operate without human employees.

Now, if you know me at all, you know I am passionate about integrating technology in education. I value my professional learning network (PLN) immensely, and I use Twitter and other tech tools to connect with educators every day. Technology opens the door to new and extraordinary learning opportunities. Yes, technology is *awesome*.

I firmly believe AI can and will continue to provide many cutting-edge conveniences for us and our students. But there are some things that computers, smartphones, tablets, iPads, social media, and even the best apps or the most advanced robots can't do. Despite all our amazing technological advances, no one has created a device that can replace the heart—literally or figuratively.

Before I became an educator, I was a nursing student with my sights set on becoming a neuroscientist. I've always been fascinated with how the human body works and can completely geek out over brain science.

I was ready for nursing school. I had earned a stellar grade point average and begun my introductory clinical rotations when I came to a devastating realization: I could not handle blood, bodily smells, or anything of the sort. My aversion wasn't just a little fear that I could simply get over; it was real. I could not handle it—physically.

My professor had noticed me making hasty retreats and even had to catch me a few times when I fainted. She pulled me aside at the end of the semester and said, "Tara, you are a very bright student, but I don't think nursing is for you. Are you feeling the same?"

Crushed, I whispered, "Yes."

Heartbroken doesn't begin to describe how I felt. Intellectually, I understood the practice of nursing. My grades were proof of that. But my stomach wouldn't permit me to implement that knowledge.

Thankfully, my professor had a heart. She wrapped me in a hug and asked, "Have you ever considered any other profession?" After a little conversation, I told her I loved teaching children. I taught the six- and seven-year-olds on Sunday mornings at my church, and it was, by far, the highlight of my weekends.

Well on my way to completing my nursing degree, I switched majors and enrolled in "Intro to Education" the following semester. In the education department, my heart came alive. I knew that teaching was where I belonged!

Do I still get to geek out over neuroscience and how the body functions? Absolutely. In fact, my knowledge of human physiology often helps me better understand the students and educators I serve. Perhaps that's why I see the astounding parallels between the functions of the human body and the work we do as educators. Most critically, the body needs a strong heart to function properly. Advances in medical technology have made it possible to support—and even restart—the human heart. But there isn't (yet) a robotic replacement for this vital organ.

If we compare the education system to a body, educators are the heart. And, just as science has been unable to create a viable replacement for the human heart, neither can technology replace REAL educators. Like the fleshy organ that pumps life-sustaining blood through the body, REAL educators bring life to schools through their unique strengths, talents, passions, and experiences. Technology supports educators. It empowers us to learn and connect, and it magnifies our ability to share our purpose and multiply our impact. Technology gives learners incredible access to information on any topic at any time of day, but it will never replace the heart of education.

Why REAL?

real

[ree-uhl, reel]

adjective

- true; not merely ostensible, nominal, or apparent
- genuine; not counterfeit, artificial, or imitation; authentic
- unfeigned or sincere

This formal definition of real is a good place to start, but for our purposes REAL also means . . .

R—Relatable

E—Expose a little vulnerability

A—Approachable

L—Learning through life

Because We Need REAL Teachers

Growing up, school was my safe haven. It was a place I "ran to get in and not out," as Dave Burgess proclaims in *Teach Like a PIRATE.* In fact, I often cried when we had holiday breaks because I knew it would be several days or weeks before I could get back to the place

I loved. I'm sure I had good teachers, but it wasn't the fact that they made learning fun and immersive that made school a special place. For me, the alternative to being at school often meant verbal and physical abuse, and, in later years, abuse that I feel uncomfortable elaborating upon in print even as an adult. In short, school was a safe place for me.

My mother and father found out they were expecting me when they were just teens. A mistake? Perhaps—in more ways than one— but ready or not, they were about to be parents of a bubbly little girl. My mother struggled in school, often requiring added supports to make learning meaningful. My father dropped out of high school when they found out they were expecting me. At that time, my parents did what most teens were expected to do in their situation—they got married. During their short union, they quickly realized that stacking one poor choice on top of another does not create a magical castle. Their marriage was quite the opposite of happily ever after, and they divorced when I was nine months old.

Ten months later, my soon-to-be stepfather entered the scene and was elated to help my mother raise me. From that moment, he became Dad to me.

My parents did the best they could with the hand life had dealt them, but they certainly struggled through many obstacles. In my home, reading and learning were not top priorities. Because my mom did not have a positive experience in school and endured many learning delays, she was less than encouraging when it came to my own education.

Despite my mother's frustrated warnings about school, I loved being there. When I was just six years old, I learned to set my alarm to get myself up each day. Even though I loved school, learning was difficult for me during those first two years. I could not seem to catch on as fast as my peers. Physical education (PE), recess, and lunch were my favorite subjects; reading, math, and spelling were not. Regardless, I raced to school each day and never wanted the final bell to ring.

In my young mind, reading was my gateway to moving out of my present situation and into a better future. I did not have to allow the hurt and abuse that life tossed my way to define me. So I became more determined to learn to read. Learning was my mission, and education was my highway to freedom.

At the beginning of my second-grade year, despite my best efforts, I was still behind my peers academically. When Mrs. S. walked into the classroom that year, she kept her wings and halo hidden, but I'm convinced they were there. She was beautiful and incredibly sweet, and I loved her from the moment I saw her. She smiled and hugged each of us as we walked into class every morning. Even me! I longed for hugs as a child, and I looked forward to that embrace every single morning. I can still remember the smell of her perfume.

On the first day of school, Mrs. S. asked us each what we hoped to learn that year. She gave us time to think about it and asked us to share it with her when we were ready. I didn't have to think long; I knew exactly what I wanted. I looked up at my second-grade teacher and said, "I want to learn to read!" Mrs. S. knelt down to get right at eye level with me and assured me, "This year, you will learn to read, sweetie."

That was all I needed to hear.

As an educator now, I've heard teachers make statements in the teacher's lounge such as, "The apple doesn't fall far from the tree," or "Oh, her mom was 'special needs,' so she, too, will require special accommodations to succeed."

Mrs. S. did not do that with me. She saw a determined little girl who wanted to learn more than breathing her next breath. While she likely did not understand the hardships I faced on a daily basis, she knew I had a love for learning and that I savored every moment I spent at school.

Mrs. S. held true to her word. She took it upon herself to provide me with additional one-to-one instruction, or maybe it was just one-to-one quality time; I am not sure. Each day, I went to her classroom before school. She worked with me until I academically leveled up with my peers. From that year on, I never struggled in school again. Moreover, I have consistently remained a high achiever throughout my academic and professional endeavors.

Mrs. S. believed in me.

She didn't judge me based on my hand in life, rather she sought to find my passions and interests. I do not remember the strategies she used to teach me; I remember a teacher who loved me, gave me a voice, and taught me lessons I will forever cherish in this life.

Sometimes all you need is one person to believe in you.

The Reality

So many educational initiatives vie for the position of "top priority" to prepare students for the future. But curriculum, programs, and technology alone aren't enough. We need teachers, like Mrs. S., who can see beyond statistics and challenges—who are willing to be REAL and to care. Do we need technology? Absolutely! Technology serves as a vital part of sustaining and spreading REALness throughout our educational system worldwide. Without it, we can't combat systemic educational heart disease—the desire to leave our REALness out of the school system because we have high-stakes demands to master at the national and state level on a global scale. Therefore, throughout this book, there are examples of how the use of technology magnifies our ability to share our REAL purpose and multiply our impact. Just remember that without the REAL you, education can't survive.

Sometimes all you
need is one person
to believe in you.

Artificial intelligence has provided us with many unimaginable opportunities. We (and our students) can say, "Okay, Google," or "Hey, Siri," and find instant answers to questions that once took hours of research to discover. But no artificial intelligence will ever be able to replicate my childhood second-grade experience with Mrs. S.

Thus far technology has failed to create an artificial, fully functioning human heart, yet the heart is a vital organ needed to survive. Every year within the U.S., between 600,000 and 700,000 people fall victim to some form of heart disease; it is the leading cause of death among men and women. One of the primary reasons heart disease claims so many lives each year, according to medical science, is because it is "the silent killer." Meaning most symptoms are undetectable from the exterior until the victim is experiencing a heart attack, which, in many cases, is far too late.

How might these statistics relate to the educational system? In our own profession, predetermined goals and standards stifle the creativity, talents, and passions of so many educators. When we don't share our life experiences or take time to relate to one another or our students, we become less approachable and we stop connecting. In short, when we lose, bury, or hide our REALness, then we—the heart of education—suffer. The result causes damage to the entire educational system and, ultimately, to the future of the children we serve.

This book is written to combat that "heart disease" by empowering educators and students to stay true to themselves, allowing their REAL stories to mold them into the vessels needed to serve their purpose and to support those within their realm of influence.

This book is divided into four sections, each representing REAL principle—Relatable, Expose a little vulnerability, Approachable, and Learning through life. Throughout the chapters, I share many of my own life experiences to further prove the principles behind the acronym REAL and how they have helped mold me as an educator, a professional, and, ultimately, a human. I would love to use examples from other educators, but honestly, I know of very few—a reality that further undergirds the drive for writing this book. Educators, out of habit, tend not to be REAL, even with other educators. We share the highlights, things that are social-media-post-worthy, but we miss out on so many opportunities to connect and share—and learn and grow. Sharing is not about airing our dirty laundry for all to see. It is about examining the journey we have traveled to become empowered educators, using those life lessons to help others along the way.

At the end of each chapter, I have also provided questions for reflecting in the Monitor Your Heart Rate section, as well as resources or Heart-Healthy Exercises to help you embrace and sustain what it means to be REAL.

The REAL Challenge

We are in educational triage. Just as emergency professionals prioritize treatment of patients based on the severity of their condition, we must stabilize the educational heart first. Sustaining life is vital.

It is up to us!

What will you do to keep the life source flowing and invigorate our educational system?

Of all professions in the world, educators must be REAL; we are responsible for empowering our future. An exponential number of young people are influenced by our actions daily.

No matter what role you hold in education (or in life), the best policy is to be transparent. Be humble. Be honest. Be you.

Be REAL.

Relatable

Expose Vulnerability

Approachable

Learning Through Life

— monitor your heart rate —

- In what ways do you innovate to ensure your students' needs are met?
- When considering students within your realm of influence, think back on a time when you advocated for a student's best interest. Do you know how that student is doing now? How might you reach out to see their progress over time?
- Do you believe artificial intelligence will replace human passion? Why or why not?

> Please share your reflections using the #REALedu hashtag, and visit tarammartin.com/bereal for more heart-healthy exercises.

Part 1

Relatable

"The teachers I remember and care for to this day are the ones who noticed me. They noticed the things I didn't want them to see, but they looked for those signs anyway."

—Crissy, twelfth grade, California

J ust as deoxygenated blood must attain oxygen before re-entering the bloodstream, educators must build relationships before empowering the educational system.

Being relatable means that we allow others to come as they are, even if they are deoxygenated—broken, frustrated, hurt, or simply in need of support—and then we listen to understand and show empathy. It's our responsibility to meet people where they are and supply fresh oxygen. When we do so, our reoxygenated friends and colleagues get the energy and encouragement they need to reenter the edu-bloodstream, which pumps trust throughout the educational body.

Being relatable is necessary for every member of the school community, no matter their role. Building relationships is an essential process to supply oxygen-rich blood throughout the body of education.

In this section we'll look at ways to build, nurture, and nourish your vital relationships, how to offer oxygen, and how to replenish your own oxygen reserves.

Broken Crayons Have a Purpose

For some students, the start of school is the most exciting time of the year—not because they get new clothes, or new school supplies, or even a new teacher, but because they know there will be consistency five days a week.

They are excited about hot meals for breakfast and lunch.

They are eager to get their hands on a book and dive into an adventure or fairytale.

They can't wait for PE and recess to hear the giggles of the other children.

They are thrilled to be a kid and let the adults be the grownups.

It is a safe place.

I can relate.

Preparing for the first day of school was something I found extremely exciting. I can remember sitting in the living room and sorting through broken crayons, carefully dividing them into two piles—one for my little sister and one for me. I made certain we each had a variety of colors, and then placed them in a Ziploc baggie and packed them in our worn backpacks. Even though we did not have all new school supplies, the quote from Toby Mac proved true in my situation: "Broken crayons still color."

Just as I colored pretty pictures with my broken crayons as a little girl, I have learned that broken people are capable of creating meaningful and fulfilling lives. Yes, being broken hurts, but it isn't all bad. Challenges often prove to be a driving force that pushes us to aim high and reach for our dreams. It can motivate us to keep going and strive for more. And we can use our brokenness to relate to others, to show empathy, and encourage others to overcome difficult circumstances.

If you feel like a broken crayon—or if you know students, fellow educators, or staff members who feel broken—remember this: You can create something astonishing with all those pieces. I promise, it is possible! Broken crayons have a purpose. In fact, I'm still coloring life with mine. If you are an educator, part of your purpose may be helping others discover what they're capable of becoming.

A Brain Wired with Determination

How do you decide to color beautiful pictures with your broken crayons?

Why do some kids overcome adverse circumstances while others fall victim to their environments? Is it genetics? Do some kids simply have a magic power and others are less fortunate?

I don't think so. I think the answer goes back to relationships.

I know what you're thinking: *Relationships? Really? That's it?*

Yes. Positive relationships change the way you think. They act as anchors that stabilize the mind and, ultimately, the heart.

Broken crayons
have a purpose.
I'm still coloring
life with mine.

The brain is a powerful organ controlled by our thoughts. And if thoughts control our brain, and our brain controls every other organ in our body, we, as humans, are capable of rewiring our minds.

As a little girl, Mrs. S. showed me that she believed in me. Although I have not spoken to her since I was an undergraduate student, the impression she left on me will outlive both of us because her care and attention continue to impact the way I interact with my own students.

You may be wondering how one teacher's encouragement changed my entire outlook on life. (Or maybe you know exactly how because you've experienced something similar.) The extra effort Mrs. S. made—her kindness, daily hugs, and her commitment to helping me learn to read—sparked a wildfire of positive thoughts within me that created strong synapse connections inside my mind. Those positive connections eventually became this tightly knit web of determination that acted as a shield to help deflect negative thoughts. In other words, she taught me a new way to think, and once I had experienced that new way of thinking, I could control my thoughts.

So did Mrs. S. help me rewire my brain? I'm choosing to believe the answer to that question is *yes*!

Are you capable of helping students rewire their brains and create a web of positive thoughts? Absolutely!

How?

Show them you care.

- Call them by name. Sometimes we forget how hearing our name makes us feel valued. Simple yet profound.
- Greet them with hugs, high fives, fist bumps, or even a simple "Good morning!"
- Ask about their personal interest. "How was your game last night?" or "How are you feeling?"

- Leave surprise notes or emails sharing how much you appreciate something they have accomplished, discovered, or simply displayed as their authentic self.

Do not just say, "You have so much potential," specifically identify that potential. Call out their talents and help foster them.

- If you are unsure of their talents, ask them. "What makes your heart happy? What do you love to do more than anything else? What gives you a sense of purpose?"
- Give them an Interest Survey. (Examples of interest surveys can be found at tarammartin.com/bereal.)
- Allow students to create #REALyouSnaps (Visit tarammartin.com/bereal for more information.)
- Provide opportunities for passion projects.

Give them a reason to dream—and dream alongside them.

- Provide opportunities for students to share their dreams— no matter how unrealistic they seem. Maybe it is through a team builder or an open conversation, asking questions such as the following: What are your dreams? What do you hope to do or accomplish? What seems impossible but you really want to try it anyway?
- Have students create bucket lists (one year I called the lists Dreamcatchers) and share them with their peers via a collaborative media outlet. It could be any tech tool that allows comments or collaboration. Let the students dream together. (Example: Seesaw, Flipgrid, Google Slides, Padlet, etc.)

- Share your list with the students and model celebrating with them when you cross something off your Dreamcatcher Lists.

Rewiring brains isn't exactly rocket science; these are principles we are all capable of performing. Right? I have followed these principles for so many of my students, and it still melts my heart to puddles when I receive messages like this one:

> Mrs. Martin, not only am I graduating from high school, but I'm headed to college to play football. Thank you for believing in me. Third grade was my favorite year. I know I gave you a really hard time, but thank you for loving me anyway. I can still feel your sweet hugs, and even though I rolled my eyes when the class danced around like crazy people while rapping the names of the planets, I can still remember that song. Thank you, Mrs. Martin. You are the reason I'm the first person in my family to make it past the ninth grade.

Do I believe I am the only one who helped this student succeed? No. Do I think I played a part in sparking positive synapses in his mind that led to a web of determination that has carried him through his school years? Yes.

You, too, can be the person who cares. You can be the one to make a positive difference in the lives and minds of your students, fellow educators, and staff members. Even if they never come back and tell you, know that you make an incredible impact on those you serve. Your words spark thoughts—and thoughts rewire minds.

Be REAL

Build relationships with your students, staff, and colleagues. Speak wisely. Be relatable and help this educational heart continue to beat strong.

monitor your heart rate

- When you think of determination, what child comes to your mind? Tell us about their story via a blog, a video reflection, or any other way you choose to share. We are made overcomers by the power of our stories.
- Do you know of a student in need of positive rewiring? In what ways will you spark the wildfire of positivity to form a web of determination within the mind of this child?

> Please share your reflections using the #REALedu hashtag, and visit tarammartin.com/bereal for more Chapter 1 heart-healthy exercises.

The Little Yellow Notebook

—⌁—⌁— 2 —

Our students can teach us so much about our teaching practice, and life in general—if we are willing to listen. In truth, students are some of my favorite teachers.

I asked my son Kaleb, currently a junior in high school, what advice he had to help teachers build relationships with students. Here is his response:

> I have had many teachers, and most of them seem like they are doing their job because they have to, not because they want to. One of the best qualities a teacher can have is to be enthusiastic about their career choice. Without this excitement, an educator could not possibly build and maintain a relationship with any student. What student would actually approach a teacher as a friend, or someone who might help them, if they always acted like the kids were a burden? I've had some of these types of teachers, and

I barely participate in those classes. I simply do what I have to and get the best grade I can.

Although I have not been blessed with the best luck of getting all passionate teachers, I have had a few who were incredible. One of those was Ms. Wright. She had a real passion for teaching students the study of language arts. The coolest part about Ms. Wright is she cared about how her kids were doing, not only in her class but with life in general. She always wanted every student to grow and succeed in her class—and all of their other classes, too.

One of my favorite things about the way she taught was that we would always do lots of projects about sharing pieces of our interests and things that were important to us as kids. Unlike many instructors who pass up an opportunity to gain a relationship with their students, she actually wanted to know more about us. In most classes, these projects were challenging for kids who were not always open about their private life away from school, but for me, I loved these assignments; they were fun.

Even though some students found the personal assignments tough at times, I could always tell that almost every student felt comfortable in her class, including myself. She made it easy to share just about anything because of her caring nature and determination to grow with you as a learner.

That is another thing; she not only wanted to teach and help students, she was also always willing and open to learning something new. It could be something new about you, or it could be about anything that you wanted to share with her. Her openness made it easy to come into her room at any time with a school or non-school related problem. Even if Ms. Wright was busy, you could never tell. Her students were always her top priority. Placing students as a top priority made every kid feel special and important. Therefore, even if a student doesn't like the subject, if their teacher is one like Ms. Wright, I think it would be impossible for them not to enjoy the class.

One of Ms. Wright's ways of showing she cared was her little yellow notebook. She designated a page or two of her notebook to each of her students. Then, throughout the semester, she would have small conferences with each of us to catch up on things from her class, other classes, and even outside hobbies.

She would write down things about you to help recommend books to read or clubs to join. She would ask, "How are you doing in school as a whole?" or "Is there anything else you feel I need to know about you?"

She made it a point to get to know every kid the best she could, and I highly respected her efforts. She's one of my favorites. I'll never forget how Ms. Wright made me feel as a student. She made a positive impression on my life. Ms. Wright was relatable.

We have students, like Kaleb, who are nurtured by a loving family and have never once considered their basic needs being neglected. We also have students who have no control over their current situation—be it dysfunction, abuse, misfortune, or any number of extenuating circumstances that make life onerous. Unsurprisingly, both types of students desire to be cared for by their teachers. They crave relationship with adults who care about them.

Kaleb enjoyed Ms. Wright's class because she made him feel special—as she did for every student in her classroom. Did you notice he did not mention loving the content? He learned the material because fresh oxygen entered the edu-bloodstream through his teacher.

This secondary teacher, Ms. Wright, who teaches many students every day, scheduled time to listen to her students and build relationships with every one of them—making notes to remember in her little yellow notebook. Does building relationships take time? Most definitely; but the return on that investment is invaluable.

Rita Pearson said it well: "Kids don't learn from people they don't like."

We can stand on our head and teach with zeal and enthusiasm, but if we do not make time to show ourselves relatable, students are not going to reach their full capacity of learning and growing.

Yes, I have literally stood on my head with six of my students for a math lesson; we collected data on the number of seconds each of us could sustain to determine the mean, median, and mode. We did a variety of activities to collect data and learn the math standards that week, and the class loved it! But the students wouldn't have reached that level of interaction had I not nurtured their needs in our morning class meetings.

You see, every morning, I sat with my third graders in a circle on the carpet at the front of the room for our class meeting. I asked them how they might rate their morning—fist to five. Five meant it has been better than endless amounts of chocolate pie, and fist meant it has been tearful and they feel defeated. That morning there were a lot of fists and ones. I knew right away we had to get to the heart of some of the hurt and frustration before we began our day. We did some

"~~Kids~~ We don't learn from people ~~they~~ we don't like."

—Rita Pearson

train-your-brain activities. Then, one of my little girls mentioned that her heart was hurting; she was still mourning the death of her brother. He was killed just a month earlier.

Heartbreaking.

Out of nowhere, I said, "Let's learn a song in sign language!" I took American Sign Language in undergraduate school and loved integrating it in instruction; in fact, we used a lot of sign language for different communication cues in class. But, this day, I decided to teach them a song. I pulled up the lyrics to "Hero" by Mariah Carey, and we began learning the first verse. Each day after that meeting, we learned a little more.

As we learned it, I would encourage them with my words: Be strong. Be brave. You have so much potential. You just have to dig deep and find it within yourself. I told them, honestly, that they might not always have someone to carry them through life. Sometimes it's necessary to reach deep within and muster up the strength to keep going. Sometimes you have to be your own hero.

That activity did not relate to a third-grade standard, but it did free some cognitive space for my students to learn the math skills later

"One of the absolute best qualities of my favorite teacher is that he made it a point to get to know all of his students. As simple as it sounds, he knew the names of all the students in our classes by the end of the first week."

—Kaleb M., Kansas

that day. Being relatable takes time—and it isn't always convenient—but it ties directly to gaining deep learning experiences.

It is true. We make time for those things that are important to us, and building relationships and maintaining a healthy heart requires intentionality. It is not something that just happens. But when we purposefully lay this foundation, we build trust throughout the system.

Our students have a purpose, and it's up to us as educators to get to know each of them and stretch them to reach their full potential.

Do You Really Understand?

Years later, I filled in as an elementary principal. The usual traffic paraded through the front office—sassy students, naughty students, students needing positive attention, and remorseful first-timers. In my interactions with students that day, I found one approach to be incredibly effective: the humble-inquiry approach. It was my go-to approach for each encounter. I'd ask the student, "How can you explain what is happening in your mind? What are you thinking about?"

They answered in a variety of ways. Some owned the whole incident, while others counted off a million excuses to explain why they had been sent to the office. (If you've never visited with six-year-olds about their misbehavior, you should. The excuses are incredibly creative. At one point, I was coaxing a seven-year-old off the top of a bathroom stall; he was just sitting up there and had a whole list of reasons for why he would not come down.) Still, others thoughtfully pondered my questions.

One child's response, in particular, stood out to me: "Do you mean what I'm thinking about or how I'm feeling inside?"

To that, I simply said, "Whichever you feel comfortable sharing with me to help better relate to why you're having a tough time today." She went on to tell me about a tragic event that had happened in her life and how she was hurting deeply. It was heart-wrenching and not something a child (or an adult) would get over easily.

She then said something that has stayed with me for years, "People keep saying, 'I understand what you're going through,' but I don't think they understand at all. They don't know what I'm feeling. They don't know what I'm thinking. No one understands." She went on to share, "If they understood, they would know why I feel sick inside and can't focus on this stupid work I already know how to do."

I swallowed the lump in my throat and simply said, "You are so right. No one can truly know what it might be like to live a day in your life. It is impossible. I'm so sorry you are hurting."

From that moment, we went on to talk about the series of events and brainstormed some ways to advocate for herself and her thoughts—as well as some behavior tweaks to make for a more successful day at school.

"I understand."

Those words have been a pet peeve of mine for years. It's natural to want to console others when they are hurting, but sometimes our words are more harmful than helpful. So rather than say, "I understand," when you couldn't possibly, offer a hug instead.

When my dad died, I remember people walking up to me and saying, "I understand how you feel. My father died of cancer last year." Or they would give some other reference that began with "I understand . . . " They intended to comfort me. Even though I knew they wanted to help, I wished so badly they could truly understand my particular hurt.

One day, I came home and told Darrell, my husband, "Actually, they don't understand. They don't know what is happening deep

Building relationships
and maintaining
a healthy
heart requires
intentionality.

within. They have not walked a day in my shoes, and there is *no* way anyone would understand exactly what I'm dealing with in my mind. The reason I know is that I've not told a soul many of the thoughts I'm pondering."

Why do we feel the need to compare our situations to another's by saying, "I understand"? Do we feel that this is showing empathy? Is that it? I honestly do not know, but it seems as though it would be better for us just to speak our truth. "I can't comprehend how you are feeling, but I'm so sorry. Is there anything I can do to help?"

After speaking to the student mentioned above, I was reminded that what we say can make or break a relationship with students, colleagues, friends, and family members. We can never really know what it is like to walk in the shoes of the life of another. Everyone is so uniquely different. We would do better to say something to the effect of, "I don't fully understand what you are dealing with in your heart and mind, but I'm here for you."

Choose Words to Heal

We have a tough role as educators; we are often many things to many people. When building trusting relationships, it is vital that we work to better view the perspective of another, and equally as important to refrain from proclaiming we understand exactly how someone is feeling. Our response to students and staff might be the difference between trust flowing freely through the veins of our educational body or the cause of a significant blockage to the main artery.

Trust is imperative in order to create a healthy system; without it, we cannot build sustainable relationships. Maybe you jot down relevant information in a little yellow notebook while engaging in one-to-one conversations, or maybe you simply listen and offer support by just being present. Trust is built when you relate to others where they are and show them, by your care, that they are important. So listen to people. Seek to learn more about their stories, and choose words to empathize, support, and heal—not hurt.

- What strategies do you use to ensure you have time to learn about your students and staff?
- What is your Little Yellow Notebook strategy to recognize the individuality of those you serve?
- How might discovering the diverse interests of your students and staff affect your approach to teaching and leading?
- How might you show empathy without trying to compare another's situation to your own?
- What are your go-to phrases to better understand another's perspective?

Please share your reflections using the #REALedu hashtag, and visit tarammartin.com/bereal for more Chapter 2 heart-healthy exercises.

Push the Data Aside

—————————— 3 ——————————

During my time as an instructional coach, I served as a human resource for teachers in all areas of instruction, assessment, and integration of technology. I loved it! What I didn't love was working with teachers who were asked by our administrator to come to me for help. Those teachers came to me only because they had to.

My heart cringed at the thought of working with teachers who didn't particularly want my help—or any help. But hey, I've always been up for a challenge and had learned to get great at building relationships. Before each of those required meetings, I'd tell myself, "You've totally got this! We are going to blow the administrator's mind with our awesomeness!"

One of my greatest challenges came when I met with a teacher we'll call Sue, who was nearing retirement. During each of our meetings, she made it clear that she was only there because she was required to be. It wasn't just that she didn't want my help, she seemed to hate me. She called the teachers union at least three times that year to complain about me. Every time, the union found me to be very professional and doing my job, but she intimidated me.

I tried to stay positive, but she smothered my optimism with overwhelming negativity at each meeting. No matter how hard I tried, every encounter looked much like the one before. I would walk into her room for our co-planning session and sit down beside her—never across from her because I wanted her to see us as a team. I'd go to our meeting with the student data in hand, a few open-ended questions to seek her thoughts, and a few new instructional strategies we might consider together. No matter how much I prepared myself for these meetings, this teacher's venom sucked out almost all of my positivity. After we'd met for a couple of months, I knew that we were not making any progress. Things were going nowhere and getting worse.

Then one day I walked in, same material in hand, same vicious vibes from my coachee, but this time I had a different plan. I simply said, "You know what, Sue? I don't want to talk about data or instructional strategies or what's going well in your classroom or what you want to see your students learn and be able to do."

She gave me a look that said, "Why the heck are you in my room, then?"

That look of confusion seemed promising compared to the glare of hatred I usually got from her. Pushing aside the data and papers, I confidently said, "I want to build a relationship with you. I want to learn more about you, Sue."

She folded her arms in front of her and, instantly, the glare was back.

Determined, I continued, "So tell me why you hate working with me so much. Please help me better relate. What have I done to make you feel such strong negative feelings toward me? I honestly want to know you better. You and I would make a pretty awesome team, but we simply can't find our groove. I feel like it might be because I don't have a relationship with you. But I want to."

Her arms stayed folded in front of her, but her countenance changed. Her eyes welled with tears that spilled over into streams racing down both sides of her face. I frantically looked around her room to spot the tissue box. Finding a tissue for her gave me a temporary escape and allowed me to serve a purpose during this emotional moment.

"Oh my, what have I done? Do I have the training to deal with what might be coming next?" I wondered. Then, I told myself, "There's no turning back now. Put on your big girl panties and help this teacher in her current situation. That is your job—not someone else's!"

Sitting back down, I handed her the box of tissue. Her tears flowed freely as she stared into space. She sat silently for what seemed like forever. I was tempted to grab the data and attempt to have our normal conversation but instead looked down at the table and waited. The longer I waited, the more my eyes began to fill up with tears begging to be released; I could feel pain thick in the air. It was obvious that she was hurting, and I wanted to know why so badly. I waited. I did not leave. I did not even wiggle. (That in itself is an accomplishment for me!) I patiently gave her space because I wanted her to know I was there for her.

Finally, she shared her story—her REAL story—with me. Her mom, whom she hadn't spoken to in years, had passed away that summer leading into the school year. Understandably, she struggled with a lack closure. You see, her mom was an educator who "had everything together—sweet, kind, and loved by all." Through pain-filled words, she described how her efforts always seemed to fall short when it came to making her mom proud.

Then, she said the line that hit me in the gut like a sucker punch from a bully, "You remind me of her."

Wow!

At that moment, though I wished for a few more degrees to equip me to help her, I felt a rush of relief that I hadn't done anything to upset her; her anger and grief were something she needed to overcome within. Even without counseling training, I could see that her heart was broken.

My general rule when you do not have words to say is to offer a hug. I didn't know her well, but I knew she hated being touched or hugged—which posed a problem for me. I looked down, my thoughts crashing into each other like a freak accident on a busy highway.

Should I try to offer some sort of advice?

Do I just say, "I'm sorry?"

Do I offer her a hug? Heck to the no; she hates them!

What do I say or do?

I sat in silence, waiting for an idea to come to me, but my creative mind left me hanging. Not knowing what else to do, I asked, "May I hug you? I can tell you are hurting, and I don't have all the answers.

I'M A HUGGER

As I hugged her, I could feel empathy for this woman on a whole new level. Nothing more was said; the hug did the talking.

Hugs help me sometimes when words just will not do the trick." And then I waited for her response.

Unable to speak though the sobs, she simply nodded.

Honestly, I was shocked, though I tried to keep my surprise from showing on my face, as I wrapped my arms around her and gave her a squeezy hug. Having grown up in the south, I know how to hug. As I hugged her, I could feel empathy for this woman on a whole new level. Nothing more was said; the hug did the talking. Before leaving her room, I handed her a few tissues, and that was pretty much the end of the meeting.

REAL Impact

From that point, we became a dynamite team. She became my forerunner for a more meaningful feedback initiative we had begun that year. I had her give presentations during staff meetings and share her classroom experiences, along with video reflections of her students sharing their perspectives on the new way of learning and receiving feedback. Sue shared these testimonials during our staff meetings and, one by one, our colleagues jumped on board.

Sue finished her last year before retirement feeling like an All-Star teacher. And, although I tried to encourage her daily, we never chatted about our relationship building meeting. The hug said all of the things our words could never articulate.

Sometimes you just have to push the data aside and find out who is underneath that hard shell. Most of the time, the frustrations and hurtful actions, be it from adults or students, has nothing to do with you personally and everything to do with something buried deep inside the heart and mind of that individual. Until we discover the why—or root of the behavior, the REAL learning will be challenging to execute. There isn't enough cognitive space within the mind of a hurting individual to effectively learn—or, in this case, teach. It's a process that takes time, and it requires some REAL Talk.

Entering REAL Talk

During my interaction with Sue, I needed to be direct. I wanted her to know I valued her as a real person first. I felt the need to be overt about where I hoped the conversation would lead, which is why I said, "So tell me why you hate working with me so much."

Those words worked for me that day, but they probably aren't the conversation starter I would recommend in most situations. That said, we made exceptional gains that day and built the foundation of a relationship that led to great growth professionally—for both of us.

Use Words That Multiply the REAL Power Within Those You Serve

I often reflect upon interactions I've had with influential leaders, mentors, and friends who have impacted my life. The goal of that reflection is to understand how conversations with them led to and fostered important relationships. What I've learned is that these types of people are "multipliers." In her book *Multipliers,* Liz Wiseman explains her research that reveals why some people are "multipliers," and others are "diminishers." (If you haven't read *Multipliers*, do yourself a favor and read it!) You can probably identify both in your life. Diminishers are the people whose actions and words often squash your ideas and make your heart crumble to pieces. They belittle you and devalue your input; they are the ones in our world who seek to tear others down so they might be lifted up. At this moment, you are likely thinking of a diminisher whom you have encountered in this thing called life.

What I really want you to think about are the multipliers in your life. Who are your multipliers?

My multiplier leader is Dr. Mary Devin. She was my grad-school professor at Kansas State University, and, to this day, she has remained a mentor to me. We meet up for coffee a couple of times a year, and she still challenges me to chase my wildest dreams—never holding me back. She overtly highlights my talents and strengths and pushes me to achieve greatness and multiply that same feeling in those I serve.

She also grounds me when I make comments like, "Saving the world of education for students seems daunting, Dr. D! I want to help, but we have so many confines, parameters, boxes we must play within." In moments like those, when my heart begins to sink, and reality starts to set in, without hesitation Dr. Devin calms the raging sea of doubt by saying, "Tara, you alone will not change the world of education, but you must do your part. You are one piece to the puzzle, and that piece is invaluable." I still think about those words almost every day.

I adopted many of my communication habits by watching Dr. Devin interact with educators and people from all walks of life. She simultaneously exhibits humility and exudes complete confidence. She is masterful at creating emotional connections as she challenges people professionally. I often walk away from our coffee conversations with more curious questions firing off within my mind than answers. She is truly a multiplier.

Dr. Devin is an anchor relationship; she is someone I refer to when considering my next move as a leader. What made her stand out from the others? How did she build this relationship that has impacted my professional trajectory? Better yet, how do we influence the professional trajectory of others?

I believe it begins with effective communication. REAL Talk—both verbal and nonverbal. When we listen with the intent to understand, offer words that both encourage and challenge, and support people with our presences (and hugs), we create the conditions for trusting relationships and open communication.

Relatable REAL Talk Treasures

Here are a few REAL Talk Treasures I've learned over the years by watching influential communicators in my life. I'm not claiming to implement all of these within every interaction I have with others, but it's what I aspire to do. And, when the conversation goes awry, it's typically because I missed one of these precious gems.

The treasures listed below are not new ideas, but they are worthy of revisiting. In truth, I often refer to them when mentoring and seeking to multiply the talents and strengths of those I serve.

1. Value Individuality

When we genuinely value others as individuals, we show that we respect and appreciate what they have to offer. Everyone wants to sense their voice and ideas are not only welcomed but encouraged.

Non-verbal cues can imply you value the one to whom you are speaking. I try to sit beside them, not across. I also make eye contact and facial gestures (I'm often referred to as the living emoji), which lets people know I'm interested in what they have to say.

2. Humble Inquiry

To me, the best conversations are led with humble inquiry. The term was inspired by a book I read several years back, titled *Humble Inquiry* by Edgar H. Schein.

My interpretation of humble inquiry is a question that genuinely seeks to hear what the other person has to say. It is not a question designed to give us the answer we hope to attain. As silly as this might sound, I think Facebook does a great job of asking humble inquiry questions—"What are you thinking?" or "What's on your mind?" While we might not desire to read these posts online, how might a question such as, "What's on your mind?" create the foundation of a relatable conversation?

With humble inquiry, conversations will likely get real. There is no telling what the other person might say, but if one is thinking about something, you might want to know that information to identify their current reality—their REAL starting point.

Humble inquiry is also nonjudgmental.

Example: When visiting with a student, a question such as, "Why did you kick that kid on the playground?" might change to, "What's on your mind right now?" or "What are you thinking about?" There is no judgment. There's simply an open door to learn more about the student and the incident.

3. Listen to Learn

Listening to learn is tough for me. My mind is constantly racing and seeking ways I might solve the problem or help the person in need.

Listening to learn, however, focuses on seeking to understand the perspective of the individual. It's about showing empathy and uncovering what that person is thinking and feeling—and why.

When you are listening to learn, pause before you speak. Pausing in conversations might seem awkward sometimes, but it allows thinking space. I don't know about you, but I cannot stand it when someone constantly interrupts others when they are speaking. The implication made is that the interrupter has something more important to say than what anyone else is saying. In other words, interruption shows a lack of value placed on others' input. So when a thought jumps to mind, pause. Allow space between the other person's words and your own. Permit the speaker to clarify the words they left hanging in the air.

Then, paraphrase back to them your interpretation of what they said. Paraphrasing has saved my rear too many times to count. How we interpret the feelings, words, and body language of others is often so far from what they intended. It is common to misinterpret the real meaning of what is being said in an everyday conversation. The reason is fairly simple: We have not walked a day in their life, so we cannot comprehend all of the REAL details.

It is embarrassing how many times I've missed the mark during these clarification pieces of a conversation; however, when I paraphrase what I'm hearing, the educator, student, friend, or family member with whom I'm talking then has the opportunity to help me get back on track—and they do!

Once you're clear on what the other person has said, it's important to accept their response at face value—with no judgment. They need to feel heard. Like I said earlier, I try to do this but am not always successful. Let's listen to learn.

4. Empower

Moving forward in a conversation works best when you create a sense of collaboration. During this phase, you can offer advice, if need be, but clarifying questions, a listening ear, and a willingness to brainstorm ideas are most effective.

It helps to have a reference point for the conversation. In *Mentoring Matters*, Bruce Wellman and Laura Lipton describe this as a third point, as in the focus is not you or the one to whom you are talking; it is on an idea, a topic, or a piece of data. Ultimately, we want others to walk away feeling empowered with something to think about or work toward.

Like Dr. Devin often does for me, the best leaders cause others to walk away from a dialogue with more questions than answers. Rather than feeling intimidated by these questions, they feel motivated to take a new risk and try something they have yet to experience. Empower people to wonder What if…? and to dream about what might happen next if they take action.

5. Provide Accountability

Of course, when you reach this point of the conversation, it is best to set a goal and plan to check back with the person. Offering accountability lets others know you care and you want to see them succeed, which leads us right back to the treasure of feeling valued.

6. Open Exaltation

Mrs. S. and Dr. Devin shared their feelings toward me overtly. They would say phrases like, "I'm proud of you for working hard and chasing your dreams," "I believe in you," and "You persevered and tackled that goal."

You can build a person's sense of empowerment by openly sharing sincere appreciation, gratitude, and specific praise for the effort put forth to endure a challenging task or process. By exalting others openly, we point out someone's successes and help them see their own achievements, which makes them feel that "I can do it" attitude. It also helps to create a positive emotional connection to the process of learning and to you. That emotional connection is foundational to building REAL relationships.

Although I had been trained to facilitate learning-focused conversations, it was not working in the scenario with Sue. The primary cause was simple: She did not think I had valued her opinion or her voice. I did not have a relationship with her, after all.

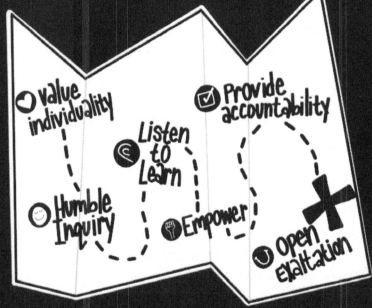

Being relatable is more than just smiling in the hallway. It requires that we take time to see a situation from another person's perspective and that we show empathy. Being relatable means that we cannot avoid tough conversations because they might take more time or lead to questions to which we do not have the answers. If we shy away from being REAL in our interactions with those we serve, we miss opportunities to see their point of view. Enduring thirty minutes of a tough conversation might make life-impacting differences for not only the one whom you are visiting with but also to all of those whom they interact with from that point forward.

Relatable REAL Talk Treasures

1. Value Individuality
2. Humble Inquiry
3. Listen to Learn
4. Empower
5. Provide Accountability
6. Open Exaltation

REAL Talk has yet to be programed into a piece of technology, and it will be difficult, if not impossible, to simulate these types of "heart conversations" for every individual on the planet. REAL Talk is a timeless skill. Without a doubt, being relatable and building relationships take time, but the return on that investment is life-sustaining flow of connection and encouragement. REAL Talk gives life and helps multiply greatness in our educational system.

Relatable versus Relationships

The reason I chose the word relatable over relationships is that we can all be relatable: We can value the individuality of others, lead conversations with humble inquiry, listen to learn, empower those within our realm of influence, be that accountability partner, and openly exalt and celebrate others.

Being relatable is attainable.

However, building sustainable relationships with everyone is unrealistic. It should be our mission, but some factors are out of our control, which is why I need to devote just a few moments to dealing with toxic relationships.

Wayne Gerard Trotman once said it like this: "People who repeatedly attack your confidence and self-esteem are quite aware of your potential, even if you are not."

Therefore, if every interaction with an individual leaves you feeling as if you've lost a part of the REAL you, that is a good indicator that the relationship with that person is not a healthy one. Yes, strive to build relationships by being relatable; that is always the goal. When greeting one who has a negative outlook, try turning the open-ended question of "How are you today?" to a positive-focused acknowledgment, such as, "Good morning. It's a great day to be alive." Sometimes forcing others to focus on the positive helps them see another viewpoint. But the reality is there is no one-size-fits-all approach for dealing with "diminishers"—which is why you must understand that you will not build a meaningful relationship with everyone you encounter. Some relationships are just too expensive; they cost more than they are worth. However, this fact should not be your go-to excuse to quit trying. Consider my point of view concerning the "R" in REAL—you can be relatable and not become a victim of a toxic relationship.

Be relatable.

Be REAL.

monitor your heart rate

- In what ways might entering a conversation via humble inquiry allow for more REAL dialogue?
- How does the power of paraphrasing aid in a more productive conversation?
- What is your conversation map—literal or conceptual?
- Have you pushed the data aside and had a REAL heart to heart? What were the results of that dialogue?

Please share your reflections using the #REALedu hashtag, and visit tarammartin.com/bereal for more Chapter 3 heart-healthy exercises.

"Just Don't Share That Twitter Stuff"

—4—

Just as cardio activities increase blood flow throughout the body, being a connected educator increases your ability to share your REAL experiences with a global community. Your PLN is one of your multiplier tools—in more ways than one!

It wasn't until I heard George Couros speak in May of 2016 that I understood what a digital footprint was. That was also when I learned about what that "Twitter stuff," and social media in general, was all about. I had created a Twitter account years earlier, but during George's "Twitter for Administrators/Educators/Parents" session at the 2016 Summer Conference in Olathe, Kansas, I hacked into it (I had forgotten the username and password, of course). If I remember correctly, I had Tweeted approximately three times and could count my followers on one hand. Clearly, I had no idea how to use Twitter meaningfully before George's workshop.

The Summer of '16

A month later, in the summer of 2016, I got to meet George Couros at Ipadpalooza. I'll never forget chasing him down in the parking lot. Okay, it wasn't quite that desperate, but then again, I'm sure I looked like a fangirl.

"George, I heard you speak last month in Kansas and didn't get a chance to tell you how much I appreciated your *Innovator's Mindset* keynote. I haven't read your book yet but want to. I got on Twitter because of you, and am a huge (okay, one-month) fan of your blogs." I decided it wasn't necessary to mention that he was one of my very few followers. But, before I walked away, I had to ask, "May I take a selfie with you?

Who knew that selfie would lead to a conversation that sparked me to begin my website. And who knew starting a professional digital portfolio would open a plethora of opportunities?

If you had asked me in the parking lot on that hot summer day, when I was taking a selfie with George, where this experience would lead me in less than eighteen months, I would have never come up with anything even remotely close to reality.

And later, reading George's book, *The Innovator's Mindset*, I reconnected with my REAL character. You see, I'm a "cannonball in the waters" kind of girl; I am one to jump in, not knowing the depth of the water, and make a splash. I'm a risk taker.

It was no different when I read about innovation; in truth, it became even more clear.

The more risks I took, the more I wanted to take.

Cannonball!

Do I bust my belly sometimes? Oh, my goodness, yes! But, sometimes I create a massive splash that soaks everyone on the sidelines. And those moments make jumping in so worth it.

July 2016

A month later, I met Dave Burgess, the author of *Teach Like a PIRATE*—virtually. It was wild! I Tweeted a few quotes from his book and tagged his name, just as George had taught me in the Twitter workshop a couple of months prior. I was blown away when he responded back to me on Twitter. It was as if I'd forgotten that he was a REAL human. For a moment, I had that feeling students get when they see their teachers at Wal-Mart; they simply can't believe their teachers live outside the school. I told my husband at dinner that night, "The pirate is talking to me on Twitter! Me!"

Fast Forward to Summer of 2017

I am now real-life friends with both Dave and Shelley Burgess, and their mentorship means the world to me.

Are these connections REAL? You better believe it.

I've met them both face-to-face and could not think of more relatable mentors; they are the same in person as they are online. I cherish my friendship with the Burgess family, as well as the countless others I've connected with on Twitter. Becoming a connected educator has provided an outlet for me to build relationships with educators around the world. In fact, I've met so many of my PLN friends face-to-face at conferences and the response is almost always the same—spot each other across the venue, begin running (like you see on the movies in slow motion), arms wide open, and wrap each other in an edu-family embrace. To be honest, many of my connections made through Twitter are now lifelong friends, and I can hardly imagine life without them.

Fast Forward a Year

During the spring of 2017, I consulted several mentors of mine to gain advice about preparing for administration interviews. I felt ready to try on this admin hat and see if I might find a perfect fit. As I sought counsel, my mentors voiced a myriad of tips and wisdom. Some of the suggestions I received were . . .

"Tara, just be you and show them what you do!"

"Make sure to know their system statistically."

"Share all of the wonderful ways you lead, coach, and mentor teachers."

One after another offered their knowledge from experience, but one comment stood out to me: "Tara, just don't share that Twitter stuff you've been doing. You don't need to talk about that. Tell of real experiences with real leaders in education. You know what I mean? I know you love that Twitter stuff, but it isn't necessary to share in this type of setting."

I highly respected the educators from whom I had sought counsel, but that comment took me off guard. I didn't get angry (surprisingly), nor did I immediately defend myself. Instead, I tried to understand what kind of experiences might have shaped how that person thought of connected educators. Why might this individual . . .

1) discredit the professionals on Twitter, or
2) expect me to be anything less than the real me?

I am sure my mentor meant well by sharing that viewpoint; however, it seemed as if the advice was to answer the questions to please my audience, which left me with a couple of burning questions:

- Do I want an administration job that bad?
- Would I want to lead a system knowing I'd need to omit a chunk of who I am?

At that time, I had only been on Twitter for about eight months, and there was no way I could deny the professional growth I'd gained from collaborating with my PLN—a network I had built using social media. These relationships comprised a huge portion of my professional learning family (PLF). Twitter wasn't (and isn't) the whole pie for Tara M. Martin, but it flavors a considerable slice of the REAL me.

How was I supposed to leave that chunk of my professional growth out of an interview conversation? What does a girl (or guy) do in a situation like this?

Easy.

Be REAL!

Interview Time

During the spring of 2017, I landed an administration interview. It was time. What did I do?

I shared my enthusiasm for education and my hands-on experiences in leadership, as well as the connected educator influences—that Twitter stuff. When sharing who I am, the term "Innovator's Mindset" landed in the top three characteristics I used to describe myself. I gave examples of how possessing an innovator's mindset had enhanced my performance as an educator and empowered those within my influence.

The conversation led to sharing a little bit about one of my cannonball in ideas, #BookSnaps (a digital annotation strategy birthed in August 2016 for students to create digital, visual representations of the text they are reading to increase comprehension) and stories of how students around the world can connect to text—twenty-first-century style. My Twitter relationships and experiences were interwoven throughout that entire conversation. At the conclusion of the interview, I shared my heart.

"Do we want to be good, or do we want to be great? I believe if we want to be great we must tap into students' passions and their strengths. We must help foster their REAL purpose. Why?

"The future ahead of us is full of uncertainties, but there is one thing of which I feel sure. Computerized machines will quickly take the place of 'making the grade' and meeting the standards. However, I firmly believe artificial intelligence will not be able to replicate the individual passions of every student, every educator, and every human; AI will never reproduce real people.

"So how might we prepare students for the future? And, more than that, how might we prepare them for right now? We must help them tap into their strengths and experiences and share them with the world. I'm eager to actively take action to add passion-led learning back into our school system. I realize we need balance, but I want students to not just learn but to love learning."

Let's just say, "that Twitter stuff" certainly had its place during the interview process. After two rounds of interviews, I got the call.

The Call

When I heard the words, "Tara, we would like to offer you the job. Unanimously, you were our pick," I swallowed hard and asked, "Are you kidding me right now?!"

My new boss answered, "No. Your passion for education is contagious! We want more of it!"

After a muffled squeal of joy and multiple attempts to get my composure, I, of course, accepted the position.

The REAL You

Relatable. Was the Twitter stuff relevant to sharing who I was? Did it make me more relatable to share my passion, my heart? I cannot help but believe it was a vital piece of that conversation. To me, "We want more of it," translated in my heart to, "We want the REAL you! You are the missing puzzle piece to our team."

I am so glad I sought advice from people whose input I value. I am also proud and thankful that I stuck to my convictions and shared the REAL me. George said it best in *The Innovator's Mindset*: "As you push the edges of the norm with your innovative ideas, hold onto your conviction and passion. If you don't believe in your idea, why would anyone else?"

Yes, share that Twitter stuff and embrace your PLN as your PLF. Twitter opens many relatable opportunities. The relationships you build as a connected educator are real, and the experiences you gain from being connected are every bit a part of you! Do not let anyone tell you differently. You know what's best; do not answer to please others. Be real with yourself and share that with the world!

Being relatable is not all about face-to-face connections, but it is all about being REAL on and offline. You are the REAL deal.

Want Some of That Twitter Stuff?

Not connected? No problem. Follow the steps in the "Building a Professional Learning Family" S'more link found at tarammartin.com/bereal. It will walk you through the basics for getting connected to fantastic educators and will aid in helping you find Twitter chats that interest you.

If you are already connected and ready to take this Twitter Stuff to the next level, and willing to try guest hosting a Twitter chat, watch the YouTube video titled "Hosting a Twitter Chat TM 'Remix Style.'" The video and these resources will walk you through hosting a Twitter chat like a boss.

monitor your heart rate

- If you are a connected educator, how has Twitter changed your performance as an educator?
- In what ways might you help others see the positive influence of Twitter for educators?

Please share your reflections using the #REALedu hashtag, and visit tarammartin.com/bereal for more Chapter 4 heart-healthy exercises.

"Sometimes, I wish they would just stop trying to be teachers and instead try to be people, that they would have a conversation and ask about our days in a way that shows they genuinely care."

—Jasmine, eleventh grade, Texas

Being relatable
is not all about
face-to-face
connections, but
it is all about
being REAL on
and offline.

Philosophy
of Trust

5

Trust is the oxygen of our school system. You can't see it, hear it, touch it, or feel it, but without it, you will find yourself struggling to survive.

—Shelley Burgess and Beth Houf, *Lead Like a PIRATE*

Less than thirty days into my new role as a rookie district administrator, I experienced moments of success and overwhelming excitement along with moments of I-might-pee-my-pants anxiousness. The initial learning curve felt as if it were straight up 180 degrees, but the demands of my position fuel my passion for education and stimulate my desire to learn through life.

Philosophy of Trust

Just before the 2017–2018 school year began, my superintendent, Dr. Scott McWilliams, along with the district directors, took all the new administrators out for a welcoming lunch. After we all introduced ourselves, Dr. McWilliams shared a few thoughts, and his words amazed me: "This is my philosophy of trust. It might seem backward to some, but you don't have to prove yourself to me. I trust you. I hired you because I believe in you. Now let's do the work and serve our students, educators, and stakeholders!"

Right after his philosophy of trust statement, he went over the top ten things we could expect from him as our leader and asked us to hold him accountable. As he spoke, all I could think about was his first statement.

He trusts me. I do not have to prove myself. Just do the work he hired me to do. He believes in me already; I can do this!

In the moments when we hear exactly what we need to hear, exactly when we need to it hear it, the collision of perfect words and perfect timing sets off a tiny fireworks show in our minds. At least, that's what it feels like to me. And that is what happened for me when

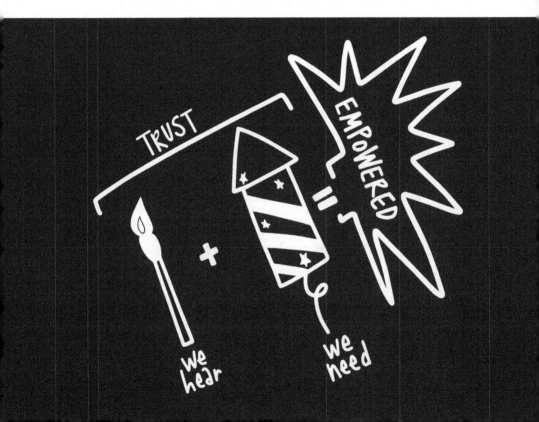

Dr. McWilliams shared his philosophy of trust. From that moment, I felt empowered, and the stress of wondering if I was doing okay no longer loomed in the back of my mind. I just did what I knew to do and strived for excellence.

The Brain and Trust

How did Dr. McWilliams' statement immediately impact my future achievements in my new role? The answer has to do with the way the brain works.

Within our brains, we each have an overactive amygdala that is concerned with the future. It is what makes us constantly second guess our performance and worry about what might happen.

When I heard Dr. McWilliams say he already trusted me and knew that I had what it takes to do the job he hired me to do, my lateral-prefrontal cortex (which houses the amygdala or, in everyday language, the self-worrying section of the mind) was instantly silenced. His words liberated me to trust my own abilities to successfully execute my job. The lesson here is that our own words and actions are influential and scientifically capable of empowering others.

Trust Is Oxygen

Understanding that I did not have to earn that trust caused quite a mind shift for me. Due to my upbringing, trusting others is not something that comes naturally to me. Being the recipient of Dr. McWilliams' philosophy of trust made me wonder how I might miss opportunities to build relationships with others.

How often do you miss those opportunities?

If you're like me, you might expect people to accomplish a checklist of items before you are willing to accept their credibility. I'm ashamed to say that I have been so guilty of doing this. Dr. McWilliams' example encouraged me to set aside the checklist—at work and with my friends and family members.

Relationships and the trust that fuel them oxygenate the lifeblood we need to thrive as educators. In the human body, if the heart can no longer pump blood efficiently, it can cause congestive heart failure. In the educational body, lack of trust can cause similar damage. When that happens, educators lose their REALness, and over time the heart of education weakens and may eventually fail (a.k.a. giving up out of frustration or despair). The human body cannot survive without a working heart, and neither can our educational body sustain life without strong, REAL educators.

The good news is, heart damage is preventable.

In the same manner, we can repair and regain the REALness we all need to thrive. It is not too late to alleviate the severe stress on our educational system and encourage those we lead and work beside by being relatable and building trusting relationships.

The Impact of Trust

Five months after being hired, I had my first meeting with Dr. McWilliams about my performance and my professional goals. Let me begin by saying, he is a master communicator. During that meeting, he commended me for my performance and asked how I felt about the progress and growth opportunities that had presented themselves since my first day on the job. Rather than feeling nervous about meeting with my boss, I felt as if I was visiting with a friend over coffee. His questions led me to share the lessons I had learned, and, honestly, I felt I had a lot to contribute to our district. He didn't overpower the conversation at all; it was all about my performance. I made sure to thank him for believing in me at the onset of this new role and shared my gratitude for his support along the way. Never did I feel intimidated or sweaty-palmed. In fact, I left that meeting feeling more entrusted than I had when I entered the room.

Why?

Because I trusted him. He made it clear that he was truly looking out for my best interest. Yes, he gave me advice to slow down and reexamine my decisions. He has also asked me to reflect on the following two questions so often they now play in my mind before making any systematic decision—or any decision, for that matter:

- How does this fit into our why—our five-year strategic plan?
- What's the worst thing that might happen if we don't implement (fill in the blank)?

I know now to always have those two answers handy when I seek my superintendent's advice, and I also know that, no matter what, he will hear my point of view. Knowing that my voice matters further adds to the trust I feel from and for my superintendent.

Trust is foundational to building sustaining relationships that empower people to be their best.

Communication Is Vital

How do we earn and build trust? And how can we empower those we serve with by showing them our trust? I believe the answers to those questions come down to how we communicate with others.

- Do we discover REAL Talk treasures in our interactions?
- Do we lead with humble inquiry?
- Do we listen to learn and not judge?
- Do we clarify when we are unsure of our interpretation?
- Do we view ourselves as the expert?

- Do we value others' input?
- Do we push others forward?
- Are we multipliers that exalt others' effort, or do we wait until they prove themselves?

A couple more questions: Might artificial intelligence lead with humble inquiry, listen to learn and not judge, value others' input, empower or exalt others? Might it develop trust with a human being?

Dr. Jim Knight, author, senior research associate at the University of Kansas Center for Research on Learning, and the president of the Instructional Coaching Group, once said, "A relationship is a living thing."

Therefore, being relatable means we give life to others; we do not suffocate them with our words or actions. Being REAL helps us build trusting relationships that provide a healthy heart; it helps us sustain life in our schools.

monitor your heart rate

- How might the philosophy of trust enhance how you build relationships with your staff and students?
- In what ways could you take the focus off the outside measures of success and unleash the creative potential of those you lead by simply trusting them to do their jobs?

Please share your reflections using the #REALedu hashtag, and visit tarammartin.com/bereal for more Chapter 5 heart-healthy exercises.

Building Relationships as #TheRookieAdmin

6

During my first year as an administrator, I read *Lead Like a PIRATE* by Shelley Burgess and Beth Houf. I applied the principles contained in this invaluable gem daily, one of which was the practice of blocking time on my schedule to do the tasks I felt were most important.

I knew I was a rookie admin, and I really wanted to do something worthwhile at the onset of this new phase of my career. With that in mind, I scheduled one-to-one meetings with the elementary instructional coaches in one-hour time slots.

Step one complete.

Then, I immediately thought, "What questions will I ask that will help make this hour meaningful?" These types of get-to-know-you meetings can sometimes feel interview-y and awkward, and I wanted the people I was meeting with to feel at ease.

So I chose to try the Innovators' Compass, a simple, yet robust, processing tool. According to the creator, educator and coach Ela Ben-Ur, it is used to "find common ground and move one forward—from personal learning and reflection practices to organizational practices like design thinking." My purpose for using the Innovators' Compass was unlike any of the examples on the website (innovatorscompass.org), but I really hoped to figure out a way to use it to guide my initial, one-to-one, get-to-know-you conversations with the instructional coaches. Even after studying the tool, I was not 100 percent sure how to make my brainstorm a reality. With my first meeting scheduled for the next day, I had to figure things out, and quickly, so I called my PLN friend and educational consultant, Audrey O'Clair (@audreyoclair on Twitter), and shared my thoughts. She spent about fifteen minutes walking me through the Innovators' Compass process and helping me tailor it to fit my needs.

During our conversation, she kept the focus of the responses on the recipient's professional needs. However, after implementing it with the first instructional coach, I decided to add REALness into the mix. It was a relatively simple adjustment that added the possibility of personal and/or professional to each question. Genius.

Implementing REAL + Innovators' Compass

Implementing REAL + Innovators' Compass is relatively easy but might seem a bit strange due to the timed feature. Trust me; follow the process, and the results will astound you.

You will need sticky notes or sections of a blank sheet of paper and a timer. Begin with the center of the compass. Ask the questions designated for each section. Set the timer for two minutes, and then allow the innovator to write down their responses. After the first section, move clockwise to the next segment of the compass. Repeat the process.

After Quadrant 3 is complete, set the timer aside and engage in authentic dialogue. This is my favorite part, because it allows time to apply the Relatable REAL Talk Treasures during the conversation. After they walk you through the completed sections, summarize their responses and move to the last quadrant. Set the timer for two minutes, one last time.

After Quadrant 4, have the innovator share their action steps, and inquire with, "How can I serve and support you to reach these goals?" The answers they provide will guide the remainder of the conversation. Then, conclude the discussion naturally.

*For more detailed directions, please watch the short video or view the infographics found in the "Relatable Heart Cardio Exercises" section at the end of this chapter.

Why Spontaneity?

Why timed?

Besides the fact that you do not have endless amounts of free time, giving the innovator only two minutes per quadrant serves multiple purposes, one of which is giving the conversation some structure.

Racing a timer can be intimidating at times and seem so impersonal, but this is not the intent for the time bound. The true reason lies within the prefrontal cortex—the worrying section of our mind. If we are left to contemplate our answers, we are more likely to silence our true feelings or thoughts.

When you're racing a timer, you are pulling from your long-term memory—thoughts you have allowed to find a lodging place deep inside your brain. This is the power of REALness. You will notice in the feedback below, some of the innovators expressed dreams they have never told anyone, yet listed them on the sticky notes during the REAL + Innovators' Compass experience?

Powerful.

So please warn the innovators of the timed factor to alleviate anxiety. Then, help them trust the process.

After each coach completed their REAL + Innovators' Compass, I took a picture of their sticky notes and placed the image, along with their sticky notes, in a file folder that we would revisit in a few months. I assured them, they might want to rearrange sticky notes, make adjustments, or add and delete items. We discussed what they hoped to see different the next time we revisited their compass.

Before tucking the files safely away, I typed their responses into a Google Sheet. Making a spreadsheet might sound geeky or weird, but it has served me well. When I'm making my drive-by visits, I peek at the spreadsheet beforehand to remind me of the coach's interests and ambitions. While I'd like to think I can remember all of the aspirations of the hundreds of educators I serve, I realize that is impossible.

The results from the Innovators' Compass activity filled my spreadsheet with so much helpful information about the coaches I lead.

Before using this processing tool, I was intentional about learning the individual passions of the educators within my realm of influence (and typing them in a Google Sheet). Then, I'd add the educator by name and school name. It really helped me make personal connections and tailor my support to meet their needs.

With the Innovators' Compass, however, I had a full document of the dreams and ambitions of my instructional coaches, as well as a list of what they valued personally and professionally. When I walked away from these one-hour meetings, we each knew how the coach planned to keep the personal passions and desires of the teachers they supported at the forefront of their work.

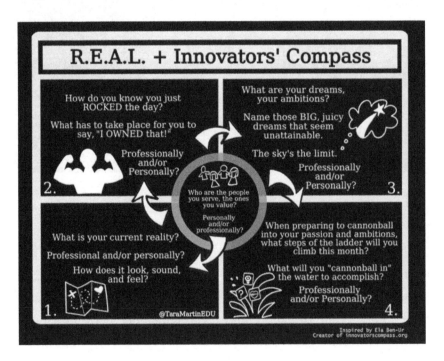

This tool helped me collect—in one hour—information that once took weeks, even months, of interactions to attain. The Innovators'-Compass-led meetings propelled me in the right direction to lead an amazing group of instructional coaches, and I will continue to use the REAL + Innovators' Compass to lead and guide educators.

REAL Talk Feedback

This experience was as valuable to me as it was for my instructional coaches. As you can see from the feedback they offered, they learned a lot about themselves in the process.

> *"As always, Tara worked outside the box on this one. As I was working through the Innovators' Compass, I found myself thinking outside the box as well. This isn't just for educators; it's for every relationship you want to nurture."*
>
> —Erica V., instructional facilitator (coach)

> *"On my way to our initial one-on-one meeting, I was fully expecting our time together would be spent answering standard get-to-know-you questions. I should have known you would have a more creative approach, adding some 'bam' to a typically basic activity. At first, I didn't know what to expect when you introduced the concept of the Innovators' Compass to me. In fact, I was a bit apprehensive that the activity wouldn't be beneficial to the purpose of our meeting; however, I quickly realized that the Innovators' Compass did more than just allow you to get to know me better.*
>
> *"The Innovators' Compass provided a platform for you to truly know me as an individual and not just*

an employee. Not only did the Innovators' Compass provide you with insight into who I am, it also allowed me to be real with myself by forcing me to write down some of my hidden dreams, which I've never articulated to anyone else. I left our meeting proud that I allowed myself to be vulnerable and open up about who I am at my core. The Innovators' Compass also provided us with an opportunity to connect and have a genuine conversation about our passions and values."

—Chelsea A., instructional facilitator (coach)

"The melding of personal and professional perceptions enhanced the reality that being an educator is a way of life. Your way of connecting our professional roles with our hearts, and devotion to youth, keeps us connected to our purpose of supporting youth!"

—Jaime C., director of student services

"The Innovators' Compass process allowed Tara a timely way to get to know me better. Through the process, it was clear that she wanted to know me as a human being, which then fostered a better working relationship with her because we were allowed time to share who we are. Through this tool, she also got to see my strengths and weaknesses and reflect on how she can support me.

"As a leader and mentor in my own building, I tested the tool out with a few teachers I didn't know as well. Through using the Innovators' Compass, I was able to see each teacher as a human being who ultimately wants the best for each child."

—Teresa P., instructional facilitator (coach)

REAL + Innovators' Compass Follow-Up Meeting

During the mid-year goals meeting with the instructional coaches, we repeated the REAL + Innovators' Compass process. After this second round, I pulled out their old sticky notes, and we made comparisons. It was incredible to see significant growth in the areas of "What is your current reality?" and "What will you cannonball into to accomplish?" They were excited to cross items off their old sticky notes or crumple and toss them in the trash. The meetings had a celebratory feel, and the coaches seemed to feel invested to cannonball into more adventurous tasks during this round.

Building relationships takes time, but with this powerful tool, you can lay the foundation for a working relationship and spark an emotional connection with those you serve—in an hour or less.

Our years may be limited on Earth, but we can foster relationships that will stand the test of time. It takes personal investment, but the impact is invaluable. The clock is ticking. What are you waiting for?

If you choose to use the Innovators' Compass, please share your experience with me @TaraMartinEDU and Ela Ben-Ur, the creator of the Innovators' Compass, at @ElaBenUr on Twitter. Also, do not forget to use the hashtag #InnovatorsCompass.

For more REAL + Innovators' Compass Direction

Watch the short video on my website referenced below to discover how you might lead a REAL get-to-know-you conversation.

monitor your heart rate

- When people are timed while responding to a question, they often share what pops into their mind at that moment, no contemplating. How might this benefit the Innovators' Compass process?
- In what ways could you use the results from this activity to better lead your students and/or staff?
- What questions would you like to add, take away, or tweak from the Innovators' Compass?
- How could this method of relationship building enhance your students' academic achievement?

Please share your reflections using the #REALedu and #InnovatorsCompass hashtags. Visit innovatorscompass.org for more about Innovators' Compass, and taramartin.com/bereal for more Chapter 6 heart-healthy exercises.

That Little Girl with the Crooked Pigtails . . .

- cannot wait to reach the door of her classroom and hug you, every single morning.
- knows you will welcome her with a smile, and that makes her feel special.
- thinks sitting in the back row next to your desk is perfect. In fact, sitting any place in your classroom is her favorite.
- loves school; it's her safe place.
- wishes you knew how much you meant to her.
- wishes she could tell you that she has mastered the cold stare she gives to the kids who make fun of her because it helps hide the hurt she feels.
- swallows hard and says, "Fine," when asked how her night was.
- will not tell you the truth about what's happening in her mind and heart no matter how hard you might pry. Never.
- wishes you knew she hides in the wooded area behind her house to sit alone and cry rivers of tears.
- wants you to know she feels like a jagged puzzle piece that never really fits in—no matter where it's placed.
- has better handwriting but had to do her homework on the shaky bus ride to school.

- wishes you knew how badly she wants to make you happy, but doing homework is the last thing on her mind when she is at home.
- is grateful you taught her to write. Years later, it's still her passion.
- when she smiles with that little twinkle in her eye, she truly believes you when you say, "You will reach your dreams one day! Keep working hard. You're an overcomer."
- holds on to your every word when you kneel down and look her in the eyes and say, "You're not defined by your current circumstances. You will write your own story. Dream big, sweetie!"
- will always remember you and all of the "life lessons" you taught her.
- will come to an understanding that one person believing in another can reshape a person's future.
- will one day pay it forward and show empathy while encouraging other students and adults to follow their passions and overcome—just like you modeled for her.
- will have scars as an adult but will stand strong.

Why?

Because of you! Did you make every student in your class feel like the favorite?

Most likely, but to this one, you stood out. You gave her hope to cling to, and she still has not let go! To this day, over three decades later, your words ring in her heart and mind.

To the Educators of the World

Your words and actions are unforgettable. Measure what you say and how you say it. The good and the bad stick—for years and years to come. Listen to understand all kids. They have a perspective, too. Be the difference for that little girl with crooked pigtails (and the little boys) in your class, school, or district.

Part 2

Expose Vulnerability

> *"She made me feel important and not like I was just a number. She took time out of her own schedule to help me when I struggled with a subject I had trouble with or even when I was having problems at home. She inspired me to become a teacher and to also care for my students just like she cared for all of hers."*
>
> —Samantha, twelfth grade, Missouri

There is so much value in exposing vulnerability, yet we convince ourselves it is better to hide deep within ourselves, that our hearts should rarely, if ever, be shared. Why are we ashamed of our REAL identity?

Do we fear what others will think?

Do we compare ourselves to others?

Do the critics paralyze us?

Or are we afraid of our full potential?

Brené Brown said it best in *Braving the Wilderness*: "True belonging and self-worth are not goods; we don't negotiate their value with the world. The truth about who we are lives in our hearts. Our call to courage is to protect our wild heart against constant evaluation, especially our own."

It takes a lot of courage to expose parts of our identity. But it is often the parts of our stories that are hardest to share that make us who we are; they are what make us real.

Exposing vulnerability helps others relate to us. When we begin to share unique parts and pieces of our life, we help others realize they are not alone. Exposing vulnerability is empowering. Our lives are flooded with fake news, lies, and perfect-life social media posts. It's no wonder, then, that the world is craving people who are REAL.

Cannonball–In Theory

"Vulnerability is not knowing victory or defeat; it's understanding the necessity of both. It's engaging. It's being all in."

—Brené Brown

When I was a little girl, my parents would take us to the city pool on special occasions. It was a real treat for us, as I knew it was an extra expense.

Unfortunately, until I was about eight years old, I was terrified of the water. Each trip, I would sit on the second step and watch everyone splash around. I wanted to swim but was afraid. I had (still have) many sensory issues, so I often credit my fear to that. I *wished* that I dared to wade in far enough to have some fun, but fear wouldn't let me.

Then, one day, my dad held my hand and helped me learn to walk in the water. With his encouragement, I learned to doggie paddle. Then I learned to go under water and hold my breath. (Side Note: My dad may have smoked five packs of cigarettes per day, but he could hold his breath for what seemed like five solid minutes.) Before long, I was swimming laps alongside my dad where it was only four feet deep in case I had to stop for air.

Each time we swam near the side where the diving boards were in clear view, I'd stop and watch the jumpers. I wanted to jump, but I still thought that was out of my league. Sometimes people would dive like dolphins. Other times, tiny kids would jump off and swim to the side. Then there were the flippers. But my favorite of all time were the cannonballers! Sometimes they'd splash so big it would get in my face—in the shallow end! Those jumpers made waves.

It was not long before my dad was nudging me to try the diving board, and I was scared to death. I remember that first climb—one rung at a time until I reached the top. Then, looking down at my dad, my fear screamed, "There's no way!" Down I climbed, past the kids making fun of me for being a wimp. I went back to what I knew I could do—swimming laps.

But the next trip, I tried again.

This time, my dad cannonballed in first. He was the best of all cannonballers. His splash almost always soaked the pretty lifeguards.

Next, it was my turn. I'm not sure what changed. Maybe it was the fear of the kids behind me calling me a baby like they had last time. Maybe some hidden bravery had suddenly decided to bubble to the surface. Whatever the reason, I found the courage to climb the rungs of that ladder with purpose. Once I reached the board, I got a running start and never looked back. I grabbed both knees like I had watched so many times and hoped my sixty-pound body would make a massive splash and some rocking waves.

I did it!

From that moment on, be it in the pool or life in general, I became a cannonball-in kind of girl.

So what does that have to do with exposing vulnerability?

Everything.

Even as a child, I was not meant to sit on the steps of life and watch everyone around me take risks and learn from their experiences. I was born to jump into the deep waters and make waves. We have to be willing to take risks in order to discover and fulfill our purpose in education and in life.

Are you tired of dipping your toes in the water and inching your way in? Is there something you're passionate about? Do those thoughts consume your day and night, but you're afraid to act?

Maybe it is

a new idea,

a dream,

a passion,

a courageous conversation,

standing up for something,

or _____ (fill in the blank).

No doubt, this vulnerable place is a key characteristic that makes you special—and unlike anyone else. Of this, I feel certain. Without it, you wouldn't be human. If it's something you desire to accomplish or know must be attempted, why are you still in the shallow end, barely up to your ankles?

What is it that fills you with fear?

Are you hoping the water will eventually feel normal, and you will swim freely? If you plan to do this thing that burns in your soul, you will eventually be submerged. You know that, right?

Cannonball-In Theory

Why not cannonball in?

Yes! Quit dipping your toes in the water and waiting for perfect conditions or for the fear to fade. Swallow the lump in your throat and climb the rungs of the high dive. With each step, reach up and grip the handles with determination. Believe in yourself—in your purpose. Try to remember all of those who once poured gasoline on your fire. Draw on the power of their encouraging words. Once on the back of the board, do not walk to the edge and look down. Don't do it!

Muster up all of your zeal and get a running start.

As you approach the edge of the diving board, bend your knees just right, and jump with all your might—as high as you can. Push off the board with great force, striving to land dead center of the pool.

While in the air, don't look down, look up. Grab your knees with both hands, don't worry about holding your nose; just hold your breath!

Feel the rush? As you descend rapidly into the water, let your mind smile with an intention to make a splash so big it soaks anyone anywhere near the pool!

In the Deep End

You did it!

You're all in.

You're submerged.

You are no longer worried about those petty, fearful thoughts—Is the temperature just right? Will I be able to make it back to the side?—that once kept you paralyzed No. That is not even on your mind at this moment. You're in. You're in deep!

As you stretch your feet out to touch the bottom, you feel nothing. Darn, you hoped to give yourself a little boost from the solid surface, but that is not an option.

Open your eyes and look up at the sunlight beaming through the waters. It is going to be a while before you reach air. You can feel your pulse in your temples from the barometric pressure. Fear grips you and you begin to panic: I'm in over my head—literally! What if I can't hold my breath that long?

Who are you kidding? You're not going to allow yourself to drown—you *will swim*! You know the skills; rely on your talents and strengths. Your body is craving one deep breath, but that is not an option yet. Don't panic. Do what you know to do. Don't give in. Hold on just a little while longer.

Reach up with both hands outstretched, palms facing away from your body, and push water like your life depends on it. It does.

Exposing vulnerability is scary, but don't panic. Don't allow your mind to go there. It's a waste of cognitive energy. Think wisely. Fight for what you believe. Continue to push the water behind you.

Look up and see the light and, with each stroke, remember:

Push the doubt behind you.

Push the fear behind you.

Push the I-can't-do-this behind you.

Push the what-if-others-are-judging-me behind you.

Push the my-head-might-explode behind you.

Swim.

When you feel like you just cannot hold your breath a second more, remind yourself of your purpose—your goal. Recall the words of Roosevelt: "Nothing in the world is worth having or worth doing unless it means effort, pain, difficulty."

Focus.

Swim.

When you feel the breeze on your palms as they poke through the surface of the water, you know you're a second away from your first breath. You did it. Inhale. Exhale. Don't relax, though; tread water steadily.

Scan your surroundings. Yes, you're still dead center of the pool. You're all in. Don't panic. Take in oxygen and release carbon monoxide. Take a couple more breaths. You cannot tread water forever; you must swim. There is no surface to push off and propel you forward. It's just you—alone. You can't touch the bottom. Your body is weary, but you cannot give up. You're so close now, and you have air.

You've got this.

Swim.

Put your head in the water, swing your right arm high above the water with your palm facing down, and push the doubt, fear, and uncertainty away from you. Then, do the same with the left arm. If anything tries to stop you, push it back with authority. Keep your eyes on your intent. Every three strokes, turn your head to the side and take in a breath. Exhale under water with your eyes fixed on the destination. Keep kicking your legs rhythmically. Hold your head steady. This is easier than before. You have air available.

Swim.

When your fingertips reach the edge of the pool, grip it hard and pull yourself to the side. Lean your weary body against the wall and look back.

The water is still rippling from your cannonball. You made waves.

You made waves!

The lifeguard is soaked. You did that. You're breathing hard. Your pulse is racing. Honor this moment. Relish your accomplishment. You exposed a REAL part of yourself, and you made waves! Store this feeling deep in your long-term memory. You'll need it. Now climb out of the pool and head back to the high-dive platform.

The Dabblers

As a little girl, when I would climb out of the pool, there were always those who sat alongside the edge of the pool dangling their feet in the water—the dabblers—and call out to me:

That wasn't that big of a splash.

Is that all you have, Twiggy?

Where did you get that swimsuit? Wal-Mart?

Why doesn't your top match your bottoms?

When you hit the water, you got a wedgie; we saw your behind from here.

At first, I listened to their criticism. *They saw my backside?! Oh my! I can't do that again.* I wanted to crawl under a rock and die. Their words instantly made me forget that feeling of accomplishment and the fight I had won to earn the next breath. I was humiliated. Mortified. And those few negative comments put me back in my comfort zone: the shallow end, swimming laps. There, I would look up at the diving boards and wish so badly I could cannonball just one more time.

Then I'd scan the dabblers' post and see them still doing their thing, dangling their feet in the water and laughing at all the jumpers.

I'm not sure how many times I let myself fall victim to the dabblers' heckling, but at some point that summer, I decided I didn't care. In fact, I was a kid who was made fun of regardless of the circumstance, so why miss out on possibly making the biggest splash ever?

From that point on, when I walked through the city pool gate, I would drop my oversized t-shirt off in the grass and head straight for the diving boards. There were always dabblers to offer criticism—although their faces changed from time to time. They sat there with their feet in the water, their dry hair, and wearing full make-up. But

I didn't care. I did not get the opportunity of coming to the city pool very often, and I was going to make the best of it.

So I cannonballed in! For hours, I tried to make the biggest splash ever. My goal was to soak the lifeguard and make waves—huge waves that rocked me as I swam up for air. With each jump, I got better and better at controlling my breathing and swimming to the edge. With each jump, I got better and better at facing their criticism. It stung, but I was determined to make the best of my rare opportunity.

Was my splash the most far reaching? Probably not. I was a skinny girl with a lot of enthusiasm, but I was a twig. Some jumpers outweighed me by a couple hundred pounds, and their splashes caused water to escape the sides of the pool. They even soaked the dabblers at times. But my limited splash zone didn't make my jump any less of a cannonball.

With each jump, I had to decide the dabblers' opinions of me did not matter. Besides, what did they know? They never even got their hair wet; they never jumped in. Could they even make a splash? Did they know what it was like to fight for breath and swim as if their lives depended on it? Did they know what it felt like to look back and see the ripple effect of their splash? No.

In all honesty, ignoring their criticism never got easy. Words hurt, but I realized I was not competing against them. Nor was I competing against the two-hundred-pound men, either. Their splashes were different than mine, and I had to be okay with that.

The truth of the matter was, as a child, I did not want to miss out on the fun of cannonballing. Going to the pool wasn't something our family could afford to do very often, and I refused to let anyone or any fear steal my joy of making a splash.

Cannonball!

When the Mind Wrestles with the Heart

Passion burns deep, but risk-taking is hard. When it comes to sharing something deep within your heart, the mind often disagrees. The heart says, "Yes! You've got this!" But the mind thinks back to the dabblers and replies, "Do you really want to deal with their criticism again? Is it worth the ridicule?"

Allowing the world to see your passion, your God-given talents, your hurt, and your heart is scary. In fact, writing this book, for me, is both invigorating and terrifying. Once your work is out there for the world to judge, you wonder how others will respond. We are wired to think such things; that is simply what humans do.

Exposing vulnerability is hard, but it's REAL. Our willingness to risk being authentic and share openly is what others connect to in us. It's also what allows us to grow. As Brené Brown says, "Vulnerability is the birthplace of innovation, creativity, and change."

When you're courageous and take a risk, that's bravery. Even if your splash does not create the ripple effect you had hoped, you leapt off the board. Maybe you didn't make waves, but you made ripples. That is not failure. That is an experience.

Exposing vulnerability is not about glorifying our failures; it's about sharing what came next. You still fought for your very next breath. You still swam up for air and had to tread water in the middle of the pool. You still focused on breathing in and exhaling under the water while staying focused on your goal. You still swam to the edge of the pool and climbed out to try again. You cannonballed in, and the experience was worth the risk!

You may never know the power of exposing your vulnerability, particularly when you might use it to help someone else build up the courage to cannonball into their dreams.

How does this relate to learning in a school setting? Easy. Teaching students to meet predetermined standards of learning will one day be (and in some areas is already) replaced by robots and/or technology. But AI can never provide the connection to innately human traits, such as passion and dreams. I'm not saying we should completely abandon teaching curriculum standards, but when we tap into the passions, strengths, and unique experiences of those we serve, while encouraging them to cannonball-in on their ideas, we begin to hone skills that AI can't reproduce—timeless future-ready skills!

Never underestimate your cannonball-in experiences; they are powerful, and they are REAL! Never underestimate the far-reaching effects of your students' and staff members' cannonball-in experiences, either.

monitor your heart rate

Ask yourself and those you serve:

- What will you cannonball in to accomplish?
- When preparing to jump into your passion and ambitions, what steps of the ladder will you climb this month?
- In what ways will you silence the dabblers' comments?
- How might the ripples of your splash affect those you value?

Please share your reflections using the #REALedu hashtag, and visit tarammartin.com/bereal for more Chapter 7 heart-healthy exercises.

Exposing
vulnerability is not
about glorifying
our failures; it's
about sharing
what came next.

Fear Disguised as Humility

8

Sometimes your cannonballs and ensuing waves will be greeted with compliments and praise. People may express awe of your influential splash.

How will you respond to their cheers?

Too many times, daring cannonballers discredit their hard work by effectively saying, "Oh, I'm not worthy of that, but thanks."

If you tend to dismiss praise, I want you to stop and think of the hard work it took to muster the courage to jump. Remember how your lungs burned from lack of oxygen. Your head was about to explode from the barometric pressure. Sure, no one saw it, but it was a REAL struggle you faced. So when someone compliments the results of your effort, remember, it wasn't nothing. You worked for that; you earned it.

Harsh Truth

I was once chatting with a mentor of mine, sharing how extremely grateful and unworthy I felt to have the opportunities in my life at that time. His sharp comments back to me lodged in my mind and heart: "Do you believe in yourself?! Have you been taking actions to accomplish your goals, your passions? Are you working your (insert word of choice here) off to achieve these things that are important to you?"

I answered, Yes, YES, and YES!

"Then, stop saying you're not worthy. People don't want to hear that, nor do they believe you. That's not humility! That's deceiving yourself and attempting to deceive others. It doesn't work! Tara, they see right through it!"

The more I thought about his statement, the more I realized it to be true. Why was I dismissing credit for something I had worked hard to attain? Why the struggle to own my accomplishments openly?

Delusion

Might this be fear?

Am I afraid that I'll fail to achieve my mission?

Am I afraid that I will succeed?

Will others question my level of effort?

Am I comparing my worth to that of others?

Is this approach actually fear disguised as humility? I was attempting to convince others that I was undeserving or, at best, using an unsuccessful approach to show them my vulnerability. Did I really think overtly pointing out the "obvious" of not being good enough will cause others to say, "Aww...but you are deserving." Or, on the flip side, might they say, "Duh, we knew you were worthless. Who said you had value? What the heck are you doing?"

I wonder if it might be fear of proving true the demeaning comments that haunt me from my childhood.

It might be simply fear of failure. Or, perhaps, fear of criticism.

Lead Astray?

The gut punch came when I considered the following:

Do I model this disillusion for those I lead?

Do I think this is part of servant leadership?

Are students discrediting their effort, as well?

Is this why others fall into a paralyzed mindset believing they cannot attain their ambitions?

Humility

Humility is not downplaying your efforts.

Humility is not pretending you are something you're not.

Humility is not denying your God-given talents.

Humility is being REAL.

Humility is sharing the obstacles you've managed to overcome and being grateful for the blessings in your life.

Humility is not fear!

Self-Worth

If you work hard to achieve your aspirations, you earn the results—and the praise for it. Period.

Specific praise equates to encouragement. Combining encouragement with experience helps build courage, which is why we must recognize our own efforts and overtly praise the efforts of those around us—especially our students. We all need others to believe in us and to point out our efforts and achievements. That encouragement allows us to see what we are capable of accomplishing.

In her book *Mindset: The New Psychology of Success* by Carol S. Dweck shares valuable research that proves the importance of praising effort and its correlation to accomplishment. Dweck describes a case study in which she and her team gave two groups of students an easy non-verbal IQ test. At the end of the assessment, the researchers praised the groups in one of two ways. One group was praised for its intelligence: "Wow, great job. You must be really smart." The other group was praised for its effort, "Wow, great job. You must have worked really hard at this."

Later, they gave the students the option to take a test that was more challenging, but "would be a great opportunity to learn and grow." Or they could "take a test similar to the one they just had taken." The results were astounding. Of the students who were praised for intelligence, 67 percent chose the easier option, while 92 percent of the students praised for their effort chose the more challenging option.

Carol and her team then gave the students a test they were sure to fail—it was far more difficult than they could comprehend. The group praised for intelligence became frustrated and gave up quickly, while the ones praised for effort worked harder and longer with an honest attempt to tackle the challenge.

Last, the team gave the students a test that was similar to the first one. The intelligence group score decreased by 20 percent, and the effort group increased its score by 30 percent.

Effort is a timeless skill that we can foster in our students, fellow educators, and ourselves through honest recognition and praise.

Therefore, recognizing effort in yourself, as well as in your students, and pushing to attain your goals is not arrogance. It's motivation to try again and again. It's what pushed me as a little girl to learn to read. And it keeps me striving to learn and fulfill my purpose, even to this day. It's what encourages me to cannonball-in when I'm terrified of the unknown. It reaches much deeper than memorizing material for a test.

Effort, as a skill, is powerful and will carry students through many of life's obstacles—not just standardized assessments. Honing that skill and recognizing when you accomplish a difficult task or learning goal is something artificial intelligence has yet to replicate. Technology cannot reproduce the pounding heart and rush of excitement that comes when humans expose vulnerability or take risks (great or small) and try again and again to meet the goal.

Effort is what we want to foster in those we serve; however, we must also foster owning that effort. Downplaying your efforts is not humility. It is deceit or, at best, denial. It is likely fear of tapping into your full potential, which will require you to be vulnerable at times. But allowing fear to deceive you and those around you is not humility.

Now, go. Know your purpose and crush your goals! With fierce humility, recognize your efforts, and live life with the intent to leave a legacy.

Unclog the veins within our educational heart by modeling effort and owning your talents (and your vulnerability) to fulfill your purpose! Don't stop there. Encourage all of those within your realm of influence to do the same.

During an acceptance speech of an award for his own efforts, Matthew McConaughey said, "My hero is me in the next ten years." How might embracing McConaughey's challenge change the performance of our students, our staff members, and our leaders? We're not competing against others—the dabblers or the two-hundred-pound men. The goal is to learn to push ourselves to try, fail, try again—like the kid in the research study. We beat fear when we push past it and take the leap.

- In what ways might you help students decipher between humility and rejecting one's own talents?
- If you give it your all (and even fall short), of what are you afraid? Why?
- What's the difference between confidence and arrogance?
- What are ways we can build confidence in those we serve?

Please share your reflections using the #REALedu hashtag, and visit tarammartin.com/bereal for more Chapter 8 heart-healthy exercises.

Empathy Helps Heal the Broken Heart

9

Cannonballing in and being bold is my mantra. It's what I do. Is there fear? Most definitely! But the more I jump, the more I value the benefits of cannonballing in.

There are times, however, that I've been shoved into the deep end, fully clothed, without warning. I've even felt a hand on my head holding me under water and forcing me to fight for every breath. Have you ever experienced these types of situations in life? In education? With your students? Colleagues?

During those moments, whether in the pool or in life, I remind myself of a couple of things:

1. In this scary, unexpected moment, I know how to swim. I will survive.

2. These, too, are experiences that will one day help me support others.

It was my first year of teaching, and I could not believe my dream was now a reality. I was a first-generation college graduate, and I had this outstanding opportunity to educate our future. I would be teaching third grade in a low socioeconomic, inner-city school. I could not wait to give back to a community of students to which I could relate.

This year everything was new. My husband, son, and I packed up the contents of our home in one humongous U-Haul truck and moved from Texas to Kansas—about 800 miles from the area in which we were raised. It was a perfect time for new beginnings. From church planting to new job opportunities, we were eager to serve our purpose in our new location—Lawrence, Kansas.

I began the school year with the zeal and enthusiasm of a seven-year-old visiting Disney World for the first time. From day one, I knew this was the profession in which I belonged. I often thought of the teachers who loved and cared for me, and my goal was simple: give the students every part of me, believe in them, and make a difference.

My class became a family! In fact, I cried the first few weekends because I missed the students. Ridiculous? Yes. I even cried every holiday break for the first two years. It is true. I worried about them. Also, I felt that being in class with my students was where I belonged.

Shoved into the Deep End

One night in mid-November that year, the phone rang at 2:00 a.m. It was a dear friend who was a sheriff back in Texas. When I heard my husband's voice as he spoke with him, I knew something was horribly wrong.

With a look of pain on his face, my husband hung up the phone and uttered words that put a lump in my throat that would not go down. My body was completely paralyzed with shock. My mind numbed with recurring thoughts: *Is this for real? Why?!*

My dad had been murdered.

I was hundreds of miles away from my family, and there was nothing I could do. Nothing. I like to be in control of my mind and feelings, and I felt completely helpless. I reminded myself to breathe, and then the tears flooded my face; I sobbed for hours.

My dad had been beaten to death by his roommate. Both men were under the influence of intoxicating substances, and the argument was over an accumulation of poor choices. The entire scene was a junkyard of lousy decisions stacked one upon another. But this was the man who had raised me since I was eighteen months old, often guiding and coaching me through life's obstacles. He had so much potential, and I feel confident he was destined to live a more fulfilled life. I was heartbroken for his life that had been brutally cut short.

I felt as if I were caught in a nightmare. And then I wondered, *How am I supposed to tell my colleagues?* They knew nothing about my life, and I wanted to keep it that way.

It was a school night, and the next day was nerd day for spirit week. My face still streaming with tears, I thought, *I have too much to do tomorrow and can't take off. Besides, what can I do? I'm not leaving Texas for two days"* So I did what I thought a real teacher would do; I placed ice packs on my swollen eyes, dressed in my cutest nerd outfit, and headed off to my dream job. I met the kids with hugs and lots of giggles as they were dropped off to school dressed in their adorable attire.

When I asked my principal if I could speak with her for just a minute, she, of course, made time for me. I had mentally rehearsed what I would say and planned to maintain my composure by keeping my words brief and to the point: "My dad passed away last night, and I will need to leave for Texas in a few days."

Whew! That was easy, until she asked, "Was this expected?"

It was as if she turned on the water faucet to my burdened soul. The tears poured out, and I knew I was not going to be able to get myself together in ten minutes before the bell rang and the school day began. She stepped out of the office and made arrangements for my class to be covered, and when she came back she just embraced me. I simply shook and cried. I wasn't sure if I wanted to share that much REALness with my new boss. As soon as I told her what happened, her curiosity would lead to more questions, and I didn't really want others to know about that part of my life. My past wasn't all that glamorous or put together. The gears in my mind grinded against each other, but in that weak and vulnerable moment, I stared at the floor and told her everything. The words poured out of my heart.

"My dad was murdered over a cheap prostitute. He had paid for her and his roommate wanted to take advantage of the situation. My dad's roommate beat my dad to death. It was hours from the point of injury until the time of death. They waited for my dad to breathe his last breath before calling anyone; they just let him die."

I didn't want to see the judgment I felt sure was coming. Reluctantly, I looked up through a swell of tears to see my principal's teary face full of compassion. After trying her best to convince me to go home, I assured her I was better off there with the kids than alone to ponder all the what-could-have-been situations. My mind already looked much like a toddler's wall drawing of endless circles crashing into each other.

After she had assured me she would keep the cause of my dad's death confidential and informed me that I could easily take needed time off to help my family back home, I did what I had done many times in my lifetime: I went to the restroom, washed my face, and guarded my heart with that thick, tough wall that took many years to build up.

Done.

It was time to sink or swim. And just like that, nerd-day commenced. I continued to live the dream with the same enthusiasm and zeal I had twenty-four hours before this living nightmare began.

I had to swim. These kids were counting on me, and I knew it.

A week later I was back to teaching and loving my job. I poured myself into my class, doing everything within my power to ensure they all thought they were my favorite. My colleagues were very supportive, and, thank heavens, they didn't know the whole story. I was grateful my principal had agreed not to tell my colleagues how my dad had died, just that he passed away. I did not want them to know that part of my life; I was not ready to talk about all of that. And, minus all the night terrors, I felt I was managing the turn of events rather well.

Then, about a month after the horrific incident, it began. I would simply be teaching, and for some strange reason, I would "see" my dad walk into my room and wait at the back counter as if he needed to tell me something. It was terrifying because I knew with everything within me that was a hallucination. I knew what I was seeing wasn't real, but the haunting vision was ever present. Day in and day out, I'd see him.

I'd use the zone of proximity and face-your-fears tactics by walking over to this supposed appearance. It was like a scene on a creepy movie; I'd walk right through it. But the more I tried to treat myself, the more frightened I became. I had lived through and overcome so much craziness, so why, I wondered, was this taking over my mind?

I never let my students know what I was seeing. No way. I just kept doing my thing and hoping this was just some weird phase of grief. In fact, I didn't want to tell anyone because I didn't want them to think I was losing my mind. After work hours, I would do Google searches to find reasons for the hallucinations and strategies to get rid of them. I found articles and YouTube videos with techniques that were supposed to help me overcome the "non-closure mind game" I was experiencing. But nothing worked.

After about a week and a half of seeing my dad daily, I called one of my colleagues and asked him to cover my class. I took a walk around the building and prayed while I asked God to help me: *Please, just let me teach. These kids need me to be 100 percent, not fighting ridiculous delusions in my mind.*

When I came back, my kids were at recess, and I broke down. Through a stream of tears, I told my sweet friend and colleague, "I'm losing my mind. I don't know if I'm going to be able to keep teaching like this. It is out of my control, and I don't know what to do."

The poor guy, also a first-year teacher, didn't know what to do, either. And even though he promised never to tell a soul, he left my classroom that day and went straight to my principal.

His breach of confidence broke my heart again.

She called me into her office and asked me if I had seen a counselor since my dad had been murdered. I told her no, but I was doing okay minus a few night terrors and weird daydreams. (That is close enough to hallucinations, right?) She shared with me many resources our district had in place for employees in need of assistance and told me she had once visited one of these counselors. She assured me it made her feel much better and gave me the card with contact information.

Then, she said, "Do you think you need to see a counselor?" I wanted to scream, "No way!" Instead, I cried. I had always been able to handle the hand life dealt me without a counselor. But I agreed that, this time, I needed to talk to someone. We made me an appointment for that day after school. No time to talk myself out of it; it was a done deal.

Counselor's Office

I was a nervous wreck sitting in the waiting room, thinking, *What if she tells me I've really lost my mind? What if she tries to place me on medication? I had to let her know I can't tolerate most medication. I can barely take children's Tylenol for headaches and only do so for severe ones.*

When I got back in her room, she asked a few questions. As I explained my story, the waterworks turned on and did not turn off for about an hour and a half. During that time, I gave her an overview of my life from childhood, to my dad's murder, to the daydreams I was having. Then, I waited for her to tell me they were going to take me to the hospital because my mind was in critical need.

But she surprised me.

When I looked up, she had tears in her eyes, and I just knew I was more than she, the professional, could handle.

"Am I in a bad way?" I asked.

She just replied, "No. You are experiencing grief and a lot of non-closure."

Since I had shared my interest in neuroscience, she went on to explain how the brain works during these types of traumatic events. No medication. No hospitals. Nothing I had feared. She even said I was normal.

"Normal?" Not sure anyone has described me as normal before or since that day, but it was exactly what I needed to hear at that moment in time.

She brought out a massive piece of butcher block paper and had me write a letter to my dad, with big, fat preschool-type crayons. She told me to share all the things I wished I had told him. She handed me the crayons and said, "You told me you love to write; just talk to your dad through writing."

It seemed a bit strange. Okay, it seemed a lot strange, but what did I know? I'd never been to a professional counselor before. As I stared at the huge white piece of paper, my mind raced. *Should I really write all of these things out? What pieces am I willing to expose?* Then, I considered the past month. I had Googled and YouTubed all of the ways other people handle grief, and my mind was still struggling despite having tried all those tactics. So I did as she asked.

Surprisingly, it was incredibly liberating.

The night terrors did not go away, nor did nights of endless tears. But the hallucinations were gone, and I have never experienced anything like that again. I was able to perform my duties as a teacher without all the aftershock—and that was enough for me.

It was strange, but simply knowing what to expect and taking control of my thoughts was both empowering and healing. Now I am so very thankful my colleague saw the need to protect me as a person and not allow me to fall victim to the traumatic loop of thoughts threatening to take over my mind. Looking back, I realize how courageous he was to reach out on my behalf for help.

Tragedy Strikes Again

A little less than two months from the day my dad's life was violently stripped from him, the older brother of one of my students was shot and killed.

Wow! My year of opportunity was unfolding in ways I had never dreamed possible. Of course, I stood by my student and his family during the necessary after-tragedy events that were all too familiar to me. Upon returning to school, I embraced that child, and something was different. It was as if electrical charges from a deep place of pain began to transfer between the two of us. I could literally feel his suffering.

Empathy?

Yes, but on a whole new level.

At that moment, I knew my role as his teacher was about to take a REAL turn. This sweet student, Billy, (whose name has been changed for privacy,) struggled academically, and I knew he would need more than tier-two support in reading and math.

Billy and I decided to have lunch together each day in my classroom, indefinitely. On Fridays we ate in the cafeteria with the rest of the class.

During our private lunch visits, I would listen and allow him to share his thoughts. Within the first week, I told him my dad had been murdered. I didn't need to share all of the details, just assured him that my dad, like his brother, had lost his life while at the wrong place at the wrong time. It was enough for an eight-year-old to comprehend the similarities and differences of our situations.

Our bond continued to grow, and, before long, we did not discuss the pain and struggles of grief, but rather found impressive new accomplishments and risk-taking adventures to consume our conversations. Billy thought I was helping him, but in all actuality our relationship was reciprocal; I'm not sure my heart would have healed without our bond.

Connecting over our grief did more than mend the broken hearts of two hurting individuals. Billy began to perform and grasp academic concepts in ways he hadn't just a few months prior. He began the third-grade school year at a first-grade reading level, and ended the year at grade level, and he also made impressive gains in math.

Being REAL with my new boss and then with one of my students was beyond challenging for me; exposing my vulnerability was

We must share
our experiences
of overcoming
challenges, because
doing so helps
others gain strength
and encouragement.

I'M HERE FOR YOU

completely out of my comfort zone. In fact, I had become a master at guarding my heart and hiding my hurt behind a great big smile. But in this, my year of opportunities, I learned that it was time to reveal a little bit of the REAL Tara Martin.

REAL Application

Later, when meeting with my student Billy, I noticed his need for closure as well. I told him about what the counselor had me do and asked if he would like me to get him a large sheet of paper so he could write a letter to his brother. I explained that he could write and tell him all of the things he wished he had said to his brother before he died.

After he finished writing his letter, he folded it up and packed it in his backpack.

A few days later, Billy shared with me how freeing it was to write that letter to his brother, and I could completely relate.

$$\dashv\hspace{-2pt}\wedge\hspace{-2pt}\dashv$$

It still surprises me how sharing my vulnerability helps others relate to me. I'm fully convinced people are placed in our life for a purpose. I know my story is unique to me, and, although I once viewed many parts of it as embarrassing, I know it has shaped me into the person I am today.

Does that mean the grief cycle ended for me due to closure? Not really. I still battle nightmares and haunting memories every single year, especially around the anniversary of my dad's murder. But those occurrences no longer make me feel like I'm weird or losing my mind. Hearing from others who have faced traumatic situations and learned to cope is comforting. And sometimes, I have the honor of being the person who helps others by sharing my story of grief and healing.

Not only did I swim and survive, but I also helped a child swim in a similar shoved-into-the-deep-end situation. That is what being REAL is all about. It isn't simply beneficial for us as individuals to be REAL; it is vital to open the veins of empathy within our educational body. It's what enables us to connect and begin to feel with the heart—instead of merely going through the motions in this thing called life.

Connecting and feeling with the heart cannot be programmed into a piece of equipment. There are too many factors to consider. Think about it: Will a piece of technology be able to feel all of my life experiences and all of the child's life experiences in the situation above? What about the life experiences of the billions of people in the world? Impossible. To prepare our students with skills of empathy and connection, we must model those skills for them. We must share our experiences of overcoming challenges, because doing so helps others gain strength and encouragement.

We would do well to share our stories. It's empowering. We would also do well to learn more about those around us instead of making assumptions. Besides, if you strip one's title, money, possessions, and status, we are all merely humans with REAL stories.

Expose vulnerability. Be empathetic.

It is liberating and invigorating and keeps our hearts beating strong.

monitor your heart rate

- Why might one judge another without first inquiring their perspective?
- How might approaching others with questions such as the ones below help us attempt to discover the root cause before acting on a misperception?
- "What's on your mind?"
- "Is there something I'm unaware of that might help me better see your perspective?"
- "Want to talk?"
- How do you create a safe environment to allow students (and educators) to share their REALness without fear of embarrassment?

> Please share your reflections using the #REALedu and visit taramartin.com/bereal for more Chapter 9 heart-healthy exercises.

Part 3

Approachable

> "I wish my teacher knew how her constant kindness affects me, and how even though she may not fully understand my circumstances, she always manages to accommodate them."
>
> —Katelynn, twelfth grade, California

My family and colleagues have called me the Pied Piper of children, and the kid-whisperer. It may seem somewhat strange, but no matter where we are, kids simply walk up to me and begin talking, babies reach out to me, and students with special needs march right up to me and begin telling me a story. No one tells them to do it; it's as if they instinctively know I will respond with love.

Approachability is an invisible trait that people can sense.

I meet many individuals that I am fearful about approaching. Sometimes they are educators; others are well-known, influential people. Then, there are times they are absolute strangers. Even virtually, via Twitter or other social media platforms, you can just feel when someone seems approachable or not.

The truth is, approachability is foundational for building relationships and exposing vulnerability. It's crucial for being REAL! Granted, our approachability status might be determined by a real circumstance, or it could be caused by a misperception. But we can all increase our approachability by paying attention to how we present ourselves to others.

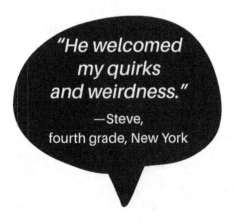

"He welcomed my quirks and weirdness."
—Steve, fourth grade, New York

The Approachable Kickboxer

10

When I was a teen, I had a fantastic opportunity to train as a full-contact kickboxer. To be super honest, I did not want to do it; I hated fighting and saw far too much of it in my everyday life. However, I taught the children's Tae Kwon Do class for my instructor, and, in return, received free teen/adult level classes.

He (let's call him Mr. M.) soon saw potential in my talents and asked me to train as a kickboxer. He merely said, "There aren't many girls in the field, Tara. You will do well. You have what it takes."

I did enjoy training for the matches. It was rigorous, and I became stronger than I had ever been. Setting goals and crushing them made me feel alive! I'd head straight to the gym after school and work out every evening and every weekend. Training for five two-minute rounds is more stringent than you might imagine.

I fought in a few local matches and did reasonably well—never knocking anyone out, yet never getting knocked out (always the goal).

Later, I was honored with the opportunity to compete in our area's state championship semifinals match in Austin, Texas. This was a -big-time fight, and sure to be a memorable event, but going to the match didn't thrill me. Training. Yes, I loved it. But fighting in front of cameras and lots and lots of people? Not so much.

Mr. M. was an outstanding instructor, and he made certain I had the look of a real kickboxer. By real, I mean that, as the music blared and the spotlight followed me up to the ring, I bounced in with determination, holding a robe over my head with the words "Tara the Tiger" on the back! I was prepared; I had the look, the vibes, and all the skills needed to execute and own this match. Disregard the fact that my opponent had been training since she was a toddler for an event like this. I pushed any doubts away and thought to myself, *I am a champion; I've got this.* I never began anything with the intent to lose—ever. Besides, who doesn't love a good underdog-takes-the-crown story?

Five intense rounds of kickboxing is no joke! I gave it all of me and persevered every round—and still lost the fight.

I was still standing, but I lost.

I didn't handle losing well. I felt defeated. Mr. M. had put so much faith in me, as had my dad—they were both so hopeful. They had cheered me on, and there I was, a fifteen-year old-hopeful—who was just a disappointment. A loser.

Afterward, Mr. M. doctored up my face and bandaged the cut below my eye, and said, "You must go out and face the crowd. They are waiting in the hallway to meet you."

Tears dripped from my eyes like a faucet. "Please don't make me go," I begged.

But hiding wasn't an option. Mr. M. sternly said, "You're going. They paid a lot of money to watch you fight. Get out there and do what you do. Connect with the people."

I dried my tears, swallowed my pride, and did as he said.

When I reached the hall and saw the long line of little girls waiting to get my autograph, I could not contain the tears. It was beyond humbling. My opponent stood behind her table with a serious face, looking fierce and accomplished. She certainly had a long line of people lined up to get her autograph, too, and her face was definitely in better shape than mine.

But the line in front of me was filled with little girls—just like the ones I loved teaching in the beginners' Tae Kwon Do classes. I stood in front of my table and greeted them with hugs and words of encouragement. Their sweet comments still ring in my ears to this day.

They said things like:

"You were awesome out there!"

"You are the pretty one." (*giggle*)

"Thank you for showing us that girls can fight too."

"I want to be like you when I get big."

I smiled through the pain, hugged them, and asked lots of questions about their fighting experiences. It was as if these kids didn't even realize I had lost the match. They truly did, they simply did not care. They just wanted to be heard and shown a little attention.

That experience taught me about approachability. And today, those lessons from kickboxing remain indelibly etched in my REAL purpose—my why. I'll never forget them. (Thank you, Mr. M., for that opportunity. I'm forever grateful.)

10 Approachability Principles from the Teen Kickboxer

1. Dress for success.
2. Even if others intimidate you, be REAL.
3. Don't give up.
4. Smile through the pain.
5. You don't have to be a winner all of the time.
6. Never hide, even after a loss.
7. Face your fears.
8. Be an encourager, even when you've been beat.
9. To some, your loss is irrelevant; they just adore the REAL you.
10. Listen to learn, not to judge.

I've found these approachability principles applicable in each role I've served as an educator, and in life.

1. Dress for success.

There are days I dress for success and face the day knowing the courageous conversation I must have is just a couple of hours away. Or times when I know I've done everything I can to help a student or colleague. and the current circumstances are out of my hands. No matter what the situation, I get up, get dressed, put on my red high heels (because I can do anything in red high heels) and face the day.

We must dress (literally and figuratively) planning to rock the day, the moment, the year.

When I stepped into that arena, I dressed the part. I looked as if I, too, had been fighting since I was three. In reality, I had only been training for about ten months. It didn't matter. I didn't walk into that ring planning to lose. I stepped under the ropes that day dressed for success and had trained hard to give it my best.

Did I know everything I needed to know to fight that day? No way. I had unexpected punches, a missed kick in the knee, and lost one of my contacts in the first round—those situations were not on my radar. But I rolled with the punches and navigated my way through the fight.

Dressing for success doesn't mean you look one way and act another. It indicates you will put your best foot forward and set forth to win—knowing you will learn valuable lessons along the journey.

2. Even if others intimidate you, be REAL.

I do my very best to stay true to who I am and to that for which I stand—this is critical. I cannot wear one mask to face influential political figures and another to face the school community. I wear one face—all day, every day. The one I see in the mirror.

In the intense match mentioned above, I could not let it show that I was even slightly terrified of this girl. I'm not going to lie: Her biceps were closer to the size of my thighs at the time. However, my stubborn self refused to give way to those thoughts. I knew that where my mind goes, my body will follow, and I couldn't allow my mind to be defeated before the bell even rang.

There are lots of life lessons here, but regarding approachability, the lesson is that you cannot turn and run when there is conflict. Stand strong. Give your opponent the REAL you. You may not win; I didn't win that match. But it doesn't matter as long as you don't back down.

I didn't turn and run, and I can't help but think that the courage I showed made me approachable to my fans. Heck, I would have never met my fans had I given way to the negative thoughts running through my head. So even when intimidated, stay real and stand strong.

3. Don't give up.

Others are watching you and hoping you stay strong; it is what makes you approachable. Guess what? It's worth the blood, sweat, and tears. The endless hours of planning for all learners, and the long conversations you have invested in students, colleagues, and administrators are worth the fight. As educators, this is our purpose in this life.

No matter if you're traveling and inspiring educators all around the world or working day in and day out with a few struggling students who are striving to make a few months' growth over the course of a year—please don't give up!

If you give up, what does that say to the ones you serve? Get in there and fight alongside them.

4. Smile through the pain.

Our line of work requires us to be so much for so many. Unfortunately, life doesn't do us any favors—so we smile through the pain and motivate others to strive to attain their dreams.

This might be one of my most honed approachability principles. And similar to the situation in my story above, I'm the one rewarded by those who approach me during these vulnerable moments.

Smiling through the pain does not mean being fake. Genuine smiles are felt deep within. While I was smiling, the kids knew the gaping cut above my eye was hurting. Many of them asked, "Does it still hurt?" And I'd smile and give them the REAL answer, "Yeah, it still hurts."

However, my cognitive focus wasn't on the pain; it was on inspiring little people to be strong and courageous. So I knelt down on one knee, smiled, then hugged and said, "You've got this."

Smiling through the pain is a determined act to force your mind to serve and not give way to your current circumstance. It is real, and others feel it.

5. You don't have to be a winner all of the time.

Our human nature wants to win. No one wakes up in the morning hoping to lose at some opportunity in life, so please don't think I'm asking you to celebrate losing.

To be honest, it annoys me when people glorify their losing moments; I've even heard of people posting them on the wall to remember. Maybe that works for some. But I'd rather focus on what I learned from that experience and how will I do things differently next time. I'm not celebrating the unsuccessful moment, nor am I going to give it particular attention by posting it for all to see. Because, tomorrow, I'm trying something different.

In fact, in the humbling narrative above, I learned valuable lessons from losing; however, I didn't race home and make banners to hang all over my high school to announce I lost the match. No. When asked, I told them I lost the match, but I fought a good fight. Then I went on to share the strategies my opponent used that were so successful and how I'd hope to incorporate some of them into my next match. Immediately after that, I would tell them about the little kids in the hallway. That was the highlight of the fight for me.

Admit you didn't win; that makes you human and approachable. But you don't have to celebrate your losing moments to learn from them.

In our world, as educators, we don't win them all, regardless of position or location. As an administrator, I have found this to be oh-so-true. However, it's OK to be transparent and share the truth. There are few things more annoying than when someone is dishonest to protect their pride. Share your vulnerable moment, but don't wallow in it. Next, share your plans for improvement. That is what makes you approachable.

6. Never hide, even after a loss.

I wanted badly to go straight to my car and leave after that fight. I just wanted to hide and cry over the fact that I was a loser. But Mr. M. did not let me. I'm not sure if he uttered these words, but it was implied, "Losers don't hide. You're not a quitter, Tara."

He was telling me, "Get your tail out there and approach your fans. They paid to watch you fight; be you. That's who they came to see."

Professionally and personally, I've often made mistakes that I wanted to ignore and pretend the situation, the error, the losing moment never happened. I've had to swallow my pride more than once (okay, a lot) and face those who are counting on me.

Sometimes, not hiding means you have to say, "I'm sorry." Other times, it might mean learning more about the situation. No matter the challenge, the solution is not to hide and pretend like everything is okay. If you disappear, physically or emotionally, it makes it hard for others to find you, much less approach you.

If I had hidden from my fans that day, I would have never experienced the joy that came after losing the fight. Sometimes the most valuable lessons are found in the most vulnerable moments.

Do not hide. Show your REALness to the world.

7. Face your fears.

I had fought a lot of fights, but the opponent I faced that day was talented—and buff. She was the real deal. She had been boxing since she was three years old, and kickboxing was her true passion.

During the first two rounds, I was hopeful I could pull off a win, but by round three, it took everything within me to face her and fight.

Sometimes the most valuable lessons are found in the most vulnerable moments.

My head was ringing severely, and I *thought* I would surely pass out if I took another roundhouse to the head. But I knew I couldn't merely defend the entire round; I had to execute. Each minute it grew tougher and tougher to face my fear and continue to fight. But I did it. I didn't give in to the excruciating pain in my head or the throbbing pain in my ribcage. I fought to the end.

There are days I face fears of what to do next to protect a student and/or a staff member; I've had many incidents where I worry for the safety of those I serve. Sometimes it is the fear of discerning whether I need to call the child protective service or just visit the child at the home, myself. We face REAL fears as educators, but we must keep fighting. There are too many people depending on us.

What about the fear of trying something new? Perhaps you know something will benefit the learners you serve, but you feel intimidated by thoughts such as, *What if it blows up in my face?* It's in those moments that you must be bold! We will never experience REAL victory unless we face our fears!

What about the fear of being who we are meant to be—fulfilling our purpose in this life? Might we sometimes be afraid of our REAL potential? I see this kind of fear holding far too many people back. We talked about this in Chapter 8: It's fear disguised as humility. Fear disguises itself as humility that tries to keep you from pushing forward and striving for more. Learn the difference between true humility and fear. Then face your fears, because others are watching you, and they need your courageous example.

8. Be an encourager, even when you're beat.

There are times I just want to crawl into a hole with my computer and write. No human contact. Just me all by myself where I can be sad, emotional, and even cry freely without answering any questions. In fact, I've often thought, *I haven't given way to emotions in a long while. Maybe I should place that on my calendar.* It may sound silly, but I've actually entertained the thought, *In two weeks, I can sit down and cry a river. Until then, I've got to hold it together.*

Why? Because those I serve need me to encourage them even though I feel wiped out.

The opportunity to just give way to feeling beat is often not afforded. I'm the encourager. I'm the listening ear. I'm the one others know they can call because their story never leaves my mind and heart. Does life stop throwing curveballs at me since my role is to lift others up? Not a chance.

There is but one option—keep encouraging, even when you feel weary. Hold up the mirror and share what you see in the one you're encouraging. When I met that line of children waiting to see me after the fight that day, I listened to them one-by-one and highlighted their strengths. After a few smiles and squeals of excitement, I began to forget about my woes, bruised body, and busted-up face. The pains of the current circumstances faded when I intentionally inspired others.

Encourage those around you even when you are beat. You might be surprised how these actions will refresh and revive your spirit. And when you do finally give way to emotions, because we are all human and need a rest now and then, you will empathize with the one who stops to encourage you.

9. To some, your loss is irrelevant; they just adore the REAL you.

So many of those little kids who approached me after the kickboxing match never addressed the fact that I had lost. As I knelt down in front of my table, they just wanted to exchange a smile, have me sign their belt, or take a picture with me. Some wanted hugs, and others wanted to know if my eye was going to be okay.

In short, the young fighters just wanted me to be me. It's all they seemed to need. My loss didn't seem to matter to them; they simply wanted to feel valued as a little fighter from someone they respected—someone REAL. Several asked me if it hurt to get kicked and if there were times I wanted to cry. I gave them the truth. Yes and yes.

Transparency is a trait we all must possess if we are going to be REAL. Believe it or not, people can see right through our facades. So let your authenticity shine brightly.

Many times, the reason people connect with you has nothing to do with winning or losing. They want to know your story—the process or what happened afterward. They want to know who you are now, having gone through that learning experience. What lessons did you learn, and how will you move forward?

What really matters is the way you approach those who witnessed your missed attempt. Remember that what they really care about is knowing you.

10. Listen to learn, not to judge.

This one might be the most tried and true approachability principle learned throughout all my experiences in this life. I'm not awesome at it, but it's what I strive to do.

Missteps and miscommunications typically occur when I choose to assume a solution over listening to learn more. I am the self-appointed queen of thinking and overthinking. In fact, it takes very little time for me to overanalyze a situation and believe I know more than I actually do. When I take time to ask questions and listen, I tend to learn more about the other person's perspective. , this allows me to be far more empathetic. I still may not fully understand the person's situation, but when I listen to learn, I can stop trying to reason out his or her actions or words and instead seek ways to offer support. Often, what the person needs most is simply for me to be a listening ear.

As I knelt, bruised and bleeding, in front of that table, those kids did not judge me or tell me what they thought I should have done. They listened to learn. They wanted me to share my tricks, skills, exercises, etc. They didn't try to figure it all out, instead they asked questions and listened to my responses.

Let's be more like the children—listen to learn, not to judge.

I lost the state semifinals match that day, but I walked away a champion. Champions win, and I won something greater than a trophy or fame from that experience. I won a timeless treasure I can share with the world—at least those within my realm of influence. The principles I learned about approachability from a fight, no less, are still etched in my mind all these years later. Isn't that the beauty of learning through life? Often, it's the most unusual circumstances that teach us lessons we cherish for years to come.

Physical Elements of Approachability

Your body language often expresses how approachable you are. You can do things with your physical presence to welcome people into your world. Here are a few suggestions:

- Sit next to someone during a conversation rather than across from them. Doing so shows that you are in this together.
- As I did after the match, remove barriers. I stood in front of my table so I could talk with the children who came to see me.
- Relax your body language. Don't fold your arms in front of you.

- Smile. That's simple.
- Adjust your posture for better connection. Turn toward the person. When I addressed my little fans, I got down on their level by kneeling.
- Make eye contact. Eye contact is powerful. It lets someone know you're paying attention. I love the message relayed in Matthew 6:22. In essence, it reminds us that the eyes are windows to the soul. There are many times the mouth declares one thing, but the eyes reveal another story. Something deep. Something personal. Something real. When you make eye contact, you see that part of the story.

Body language and physical approach are seen and felt by others. What does your body language say to those you approach?

Heart-to-Heart Approachability

Aside from the physical aspects of approachability, there are also heart-to-heart moments that are more felt and less seen—when the heart of one individual speaks to the heart of another. It's strange, but those around you can tell if you are genuine and approachable, or if you are far from receptive.

I believe children are a perfect judge of this character trait. Students feel when a teacher is warm and cordial, as well as when they are intimidating. The teacher doesn't even have to interact much with a child for them to determine whether or not they feel comfortable addressing her, which is why approachability is often a heart conversation. When the heart speaks, those full of compassion and empathy hear it. Indeed, this is somewhat a mystery, but it is true nonetheless.

Something worthy of mentioning here is that heart-to-heart approachability can also be felt virtually. Be it Twitter chats or reading an educator's blog, I can usually tell when I'm going to connect with a particular individual. I absolutely love it when I meet members of my PLN face-to-face for the first time, and they run up and hug me— some have nearly picked me up off the floor. That does not just happen. These people live and breathe the A in REAL approachability, and it is felt by those within their physical and virtual influence.

If approachability is seen and felt, face-to-face and virtually, how do we attain or retain this trait?

Be a servant leader. And be REAL. Be you. Don't pretend to be something you are not. I think it's essential for us to be mindful that we will need to expend a significant amount of energy to prove our accessibility.

We must be intentional and share our compassion with others. Those within our realm of influence do not expect us to understand their circumstance. They simply want to feel that heart-to-heart connection and our REAL desire to see the situation from their point of view. When we seek to view the details from another's perspective, empathy is birthed. And when we are empathetic, we will be approachable.

> "My favorite teacher made me feel like I was special, like I could achieve anything I wanted to if I tried. She treated me like I was important and that I was going to do something significant in the world."
>
> —Angela, tenth grade, California

monitor your heart rate

- How do you approach those within your realm of influence?
- How might others describe your accessibility?
- What's your brand? What do you hope others see in you? Why?
- How might those you serve answer these two questions, "Is your leader approachable? How do you know?"

Please share your reflections using the #REALedu and visit taramartin.com/bereal for more Chapter 10 heart-healthy exercises.

Drive-Bys

Whether it is instructional coaching or simply coaching someone around me through life, empowering those I serve is a significant part of the REAL me.

When I think back to my childhood, I was often coaching those around me: my friends, my family, myself. I participated in as many extracurricular activities as possible. The busier I was, the less I had to face my discouraging home life.

I spent the majority of my after-school hours playing sports, which meant I had the influence of several coaches in my life. I would watch their every move and learned which types of leadership helped me thrive—and which ones seemed to stunt my growth. And when I served as an instructional coach, and later as a mentor to coaches, I discovered a remarkable number of parallels between coaching sports and life and instructional coaching; for example, whether it is becoming a better batter (or hitter) in softball or a stronger math teacher, the goal is similar—a coach must recognize and assist in fine-tuning the current skills and strengths of an individual while guiding them to attain new skill levels and reach new goals. Coaches cannot force the growth to occur in those they serve, but they can guide and prompt them to stretch their thinking, which increases the desire to grow as an athlete or a professional. Coaching and mentoring is still one of my favorite parts of my job.

Building relationships with the coaches and helping them gain an understanding of the art of the coaching role is central to my work. It requires time, which is why we met monthly for three hours of professional development. But one of the approachability habits I implemented during the first year of this administrative role took comparatively little time per person and proved to be exceptionally effective: weekly drive-bys.

Drive-bys were short scheduled blocks of time when I visited the instructional coaches I mentored and supervised—on their turf. The meetings were quick and left lasting impressions. During these visits, I would simply do whatever the instructional coach was doing at that time. I'd place myself right in the middle of their daily world. Sometimes I'd hold their hand and help them through a tough time, and other times we would plan their next steps to change the world. There was no set agenda, and most times I did not bring anything with me. I want them to know I'm available; I'm approachable.

The setting of these meetings varied from week to week. Sometimes the coach and I would be opening milk for little people during lunch duty, and other times we were giving hugs in the hall as students walked to their next class. No matter the setting, the REAL talk made these meetings meaningful.

There is something about getting on the level of the one whom you're encouraging that tears down communication barriers. It compares to the physical element I mentioned in my kickboxing experience—kneeling down in front of the table that day let the kids know I was one of them. We're in this together. Drive-bys felt much the same.

In the world the coaches lived in daily, I could honestly gauge their individual needs. In fact, I learned a lot from these quick meetings, and many times we would schedule follow-up meetings based on the needs that presented themselves during those encounters.

Coach the Coach

It never failed that the visits would present coach-the-coach moments.

One morning, for example, I stopped in for a drive-by with Gracie (name disguised for confidentiality purposes). Gracie was a stellar first-year instructional coach and crushing her goals in this new role. She shared with me that she had a novice teacher who was struggling in all areas of teaching. From classroom management to delivery of content, nothing seemed to be working. She said her principal and the colleagues of the teacher had noticed. "My principal wanted me to help with student achievement, and it's awful, Tara! I don't know what to do."

I couldn't help but ask, "How is the teacher feeling? How is she responding to this?"

Gracie said, "I've entered my conversations with her using humble inquiry just like you've taught us. She has expressed how she isn't eating or sleeping, and she often tells me how overly stressed she feels. The last time we talked she was in tears and said she doesn't think she can do this job."

I coached the coach, saying, "Gracie, we can't push her over the edge. We must discover her strengths, her passions, her why. Then you and the teacher need to brainstorm one thing she can do during the next two weeks. Maybe she can try honing in on behavior-specific praise for each student and set a classroom goal as reinforcement.

"Meanwhile, you can do the same thing for her; for example, give her sticky notes of praise when you see her giving behavior-specific praise to her students. Then, as you notice this behavior repeatedly, you drop her favorite candy bar in her teacher mailbox with a note stating why. We have to model what we preach. It's huge.

"Also, we must remember, teachers are humans first. She's broken right now, and we must build her up. Now isn't the time to focus on deep instructional shifts. Now is the time to focus on behaviors, because she has a real need, as do her students."

Gracie nodded and said, "But my principal is worried about the kids."

"This plan might take care of both concerns," I responded. "If the classroom culture begins to feel safe and becomes a place where students are praised for positive behavior, the management has a better chance of taking a turn for the better. You guys might want to add a team-effort goal for the whole class—a classroom positive reinforcement reward. Then the kids will have a reason to work together.

"Also, if the teacher begins to recognize the small successes you point out to her, she will hopefully start to sleep and eat again. That's sure to free up more of her cognitive energy to teach the content more thoroughly.

"None of this will work, however, if we are not consistent. In fact, you may have to go slow to go fast, but stay consistent. She needs you right now more than ever. We cannot turn a blind eye and ignore the situation. Face it head-on, and plan to help her succeed.

As our conversation continued, I could tell Gracie was still a little frustrated with the fact that the students were suffering because of the teacher's behavior. So I shared how I often try to remain approachable in situations like this one: "Gracie, think back to a low time in your life—have you ever experienced that feeling of complete defeat? Helplessness? For me, it was when my dad was murdered. I try to think back to my feelings during that time. It has helped me remember when people are feeling worthless, they have to be built up before they can do the cognitive work of their job.

"It's a lot like how you used to deal with the children in your classroom. You listened to learn. Why were they feeling so defeated? What's the core of the problem? Then you sought to find ways to build them up."

Gracie immediately had tears in her eyes and said, "Yes, I can remember a time when I felt defeated. Lost. A sense of worthlessness. It was when my dad drowned."

I hugged her and, just like that, our hearts spoke to each other. No words.

A few seconds later, I asked, "Did you feel that? That connection is the heart-to-heart approachability this teacher needs from you. Allow your heart to speak to her heart—like ours just did. It sounds silly, but it's a level of compassion that needs no words. We may never know exactly what she is facing, but we know she's struggling deep down. Gracie, she needs a coach, and you're the one for the job. You've got this."

And all of that happened in a thirty-minute drive-by visit. The chances of that incident being brought up in our scheduled coaching meeting was highly unlikely. However, in the moment, on Gracie's turf, it was a safe place to approach the topic.

Most of the time, my drive-bys were spent listening to the instructional coaches and providing in-the-moment coaching for the coach;

however, there were times when other teachers would join in on our conversations. One particular encounter stands out to me.

I had received a text from the coach that morning saying she'd like to bring one of their support teachers in on our drive-by meeting. She said, "Tara, I think you might have better answers for her."

When I got to their building, we found a place to talk together, and the support teacher shared that she was worried about a student who had been receiving academic interventions for more than a year and was making no gains. She explained that the intervention they had provided resulted in flat-line data; the student seemed completely disengaged and couldn't care less about school.

The support teacher shared many of her perceptions of the student's home life and how she felt this had a huge impact on this child's learning.

I listened for several minutes, then challenged them with a simple question: "If we know what we are doing isn't working and has not worked for quite some time, what have we done or will we do differently going forward?"

The support teacher said, "We don't have any programs for reaching her, and if we do, I don't think I'm trained to use them."

These are the moments I have to practice what I preach. I needed to lead in the moment and not judge. I knew my coach was watching my every move, learning from me, so I decided to share my thoughts through my story of how Mrs. S. helped me. She didn't use a program to reach me; she loved me. She gave me a snack. She made me feel important. And she taught me to read. I'll never forget Mrs. S.

With tears in my eyes, I asked, "Do you think this student might need a little love? Someone to believe in her? If you feel as though she is capable academically, but she is not performing, do you think we are trying to meet the wrong need?"

The support teacher looked at me and said, "I've never really thought about it like that. I grew up in a loving home with a family who valued education. The thought of a student just needing love to learn seems somewhat foreign. Do you really think that might be all she needs?"

I told her I could not possibly know what was going on in that student's world, but what would it hurt to try a little extra love? This student was in the sixth grade at the time and would enter middle school the next year; we had to reach her *now*.

Why was this support teacher open and honest with me during the drive-by meeting?

I can't help but believe it's because I came into her world.

I sat beside her and heard to her concern.

And I listened to learn and not to judge—as hard as that might have been.

Approachability. It's huge. It's key to being REAL.

Drive-By Impact

I didn't have to spend endless hours building relationships before having these drive-by visits. In fact, the drive-bys became the approachability avenue that allowed me to foster relationships with the coaches as well as other staff members around the district. As the year closed in around us, the conversations became more and more REAL with each encounter.

The drive-by meetings took up two full mornings on my calendar each week. It was tough to keep that time protected, but I knew this simple fact: We make time for what's most important to us. So I strived to keep these appointments sacred. While the time constraint was cumbersome, these short meetings made a great impact on the bigger picture. Most of all they had a significant return on investment;

the time was well spent because it helped me to reach my why—my purpose in this life.

During drive-by moments, others often feel an emotional connection. They see our willingness to make ourselves available. They begin to trust us when we listen to learn and not judge. And they appreciate us encouraging them to keep fighting in the heat of the battle. It's during these heart-to-heart moments we prove our approachability.

- What drive-by moments do you make time for in your everyday practice?
- What might be some of the many benefits of kneeling down by a student's desk to ask how they are feeling, what's on their mind, a smile in the hallway, or possibly a simple hug when words just won't work?

Please share your reflections using the #REALedu and taramartin.com/bereal for more Chapter 11 heart-healthy exercises.

Parent–Teacher Heart–to–Heart

12

I was in my second year of teaching in a school with a diverse community of students. Our Title-One school served nearly 80 percent of our student body free and reduced lunches. Our population was not only made up of multiple races but a variety of learning abilities, as well.

After year one, I was finally beginning to understand my role as a teacher and had investigated better ways to build relationships and involve the parents in a partnership approach. I had made up my mind to do what it took to be approachable to the students and their families. I needed to keep the parents in the loop of what was happening in our classroom. (This was long before Seesaw or any of our current parent-to-home communication apps.) I knew communication was key to being approachable and showing the parents I valued their contribution to this learning process.

At first, I tried writing weekly newsletters and was quickly informed that two of the parents could not read. Making phone calls home to share good news was a part of our school's positive-behavior support plan, but it proved a bit challenging at times because many of our families did not have working phones. Determined, I started making house calls to share the positive reports as well as the "areas of improvement" of my students.

Danny was one of my students who was as adorable as a third grader could be. His big brown eyes melted me. Every now and then, I'd see them twinkle when he decided to smile; it wasn't too often but happened enough to turn my heart into a pile of mush. Danny struggled behaviorally, but this was not surprising because his dad had recently been sentenced to prison. At eight years old, Danny was the man of the household and felt a responsibility to care for his mom and two little brothers. Sad but true.

Less than Approachable

Danny was a fighter—in more ways than one. He was as stubborn as a mule and was always picking a fight with anyone and everyone who even so much as looked at him crossways. He repelled other students from walking near him. He was very bright academically. Unmotivated, but brilliant.

Sharing heart-to-heart approachability conversations was how Danny and I communicated for a good part of that first month of the school year. We had worked out a positive behavior plan for Danny, and he began receiving positive trips to the principal's office when he made good choices throughout the day. Words of affirmation spoke his love language for learning. Danny's facial expression didn't let on that my comments made him happy, but he often referenced them in his daily journal. I learned quickly that this child needed a lot of atta boys deposited into his little heart and mind.

The plan had been in place for a few weeks, and it was time to make a positive behavior call home for Danny—which meant a house call because his mom didn't have a working phone or computer. My principal and I went to his house to share the great news: Danny had a fabulous week with no fights! That was quite an accomplishment for my little buddy.

Surprise House Call

As we walked up, we noticed the car in the driveway running, but it did not appear to have anyone in it. We both looked at each other with a look of, "That's strange," but we continued up the walk. When we knocked on the door, Danny nervously answered with his little brothers in tow. "My mom is busy!" We told him why we were there; we wanted to share how his behavior had been stellar that week—with no fights! We went on about how proud we were of his success.

He looked unsettled and asked if we could come back the next day. I knelt down, smiled and assured him this was a positive visit so he need not be afraid. He still looked anxious and peered toward the car. Then he told us that he wanted his mom to hear the positive news, but she was not available.

After a brief discussion, we told him we would revisit the next day.

When we turned to walk away, out hopped his mom from the backseat of the running car with nothing but a sheet wrapped around her.

When I looked back at the car, the man in the back seat (wearing no shirt) nodded and smiled at me. Slowly my mind put together the pieces of what I was seeing: She had been with a man in the backseat and was only wearing a sheet.

My jaw nearly hit the ground!

I closed my mouth quickly and reminded myself to remain approachable. *Who am I to judge anyway?* Well aware that my facial expressions can get me in trouble, I swallowed hard and intentionally kept my face in check.

She greeted my principal and me right there on the sidewalk while wearing a sheet. Trying to act as if everything was completely normal, I told her what an outstanding job Danny was doing in my class and how he had made significant gains behaviorally and academically. We told her how he earned a positive report home because he completed an entire week with no fights or threats to other students.

She was so appreciative and seemed to not know what to say. She wrapped me in a big hug and thanked me for loving her boy. While we stood there, me in my professional attire, her wrapped in a sheet—as wild as it might seem—I think our hearts spoke to each other. It was in that moment, I knew we would work together to help her son succeed.

Approachability and Building Relationships

I made a few more follow-up house calls to visit with Danny's mom, Gail. There were days I sat on the floor of their empty living room and listened to her tell me how this wasn't her fairytale dream. She embarrassingly shared how this life was not what she had pictured, but her poor choices just seemed to cause a deep hole in her life and she could not get out of the hole that she had dug.

She often told me, "I'm doing the best I can." And she was. She worked two jobs to make ends meet, one of which I had interrupted during that first visit. She truly wanted her kids to succeed in life.

My next house call was right before the Thanksgiving break. I had collected eight vouchers for a fully cooked Thanksgiving meal provided by our local supermarket for families in need. I had already given out several vouchers to the families of my students living in substandard conditions and in need of a helping hand.

During my visit with Danny's mom, I offered her one of the vouchers. I even offered to pick up the meal and bring it to their house if needed. She insisted that she would work extra to provide her family a meal for Thanksgiving, but I couldn't help but allow the tears to leak from my eyes.

"Gail, you don't have to 'work' extra like that for this meal. I understand it makes good money, but I want to help."

She hugged me for what seemed like forever while we both cried. Once again, empathy seeped from my heart to hers. I didn't really understand what it was like to live her life, but I could feel her pain. Even though I had grown up in adverse conditions, their circumstances troubled me deeply.

To make a long story short, later that year, Gail was able to successfully find a job that better met the needs of her family with just a little bit of assistance from government funding. The smile on her face when she told me about her new job—one that she was proud of—was priceless.

Heart-to-Heart

I'll never forget the experience of my heart-to-heart encounters with Gail. She needed someone to understand that she never intended life to turn out the way it had. She needed someone to believe that this was not her end goal. And, despite her often harsh tone, she truly had a big heart and wanted what was best for her children.

Danny succeeded in school and became a first-generation high school graduate and college student. I honestly cannot wait to hear how Danny's story continues to unfold. He is still a fighter, but in all the right ways.

Our students' parents need to know they are an essential part in their children's success at school. They need to feel as if we are in partnership with them. Creating that bond requires that we must to listen to learn without judgment. They need us to be approachable, as do their students. This type of connection is personal, and it goes beyond providing engaging activities for students in the classroom or on family night. As a PIRATE teacher and administrator, I believe wholeheartedly in creating memorable experiences for our students, but if we want those experiences to mean something for years to come, we must show ourselves approachable to the stakeholders of the school community, as well as the students. It could be life changing for all involved.

Want to know what it means to be a PIRATE educator?
Check out #TLAP and #LeadLAP on Twitter.

In truth, family engagement has changed me. My experience with Danny and Gail helped me understand that what we see may not accurately represent the current reality. This realization, nor that relationship, would never have occurred had I not allowed myself to join their world and apply the approachability principles of the kickboxer. And just for the record, I believe no programmed robot or artificial intelligence would ever be able to feel the emotional connection I had with this family. Approachability principles require compassion and a REAL heart.

Be approachable. Be REAL.

monitor your heart rate

- In what ways do you ensure you connect with the school stakeholders?
- What's your go-to parent/community communication method?
- In what ways does your communication allow community members to share their REALness?
- Describe a positive heart-to-heart moment you have had with a parent or community stakeholder. How did this connection affect the education of the students involved?

Please share your reflections using the #REALedu hashtag, and visit tarammartin.com/bereal for more Chapter 12 heart-healthy exercises.

"My favorite teacher made me feel extra supported because she always said, 'You are a light in the world.'"

—Lucas, second grade, Oregon

Deep. Personal. R.e.a.l.

LISTEN TO LEARN

stay consistant

build them up

" ... our hearts spoke to each other. No words. "

DRIVE-BYS AHEAD

approachable

Reachable

YOU GOT THIS!
Never Hide
TARA THE TIGER
APPROACHABLE
Slow to Go fast
R.E.A.L. approachability
R.E.A.L. partnership
R.E.A.L. words
Lead in the moment and do not judge!
R.E.A.L. empathy
Heart and Mind
team effort

Dear Future Administrator Me

Here are a few tips I hope you never forget as you embark upon this new journey of administration. (This is a letter I wrote to myself before my first administration job.)

Build relationships *first*!

Listen to teachers, students, and the school community. Their voices need to not only be heard but valued.

Be transparent.

Turn the spotlight on others and let them shine; it's a direct reflection of outstanding leadership.

MODEL! Walk the talk. LIVE it. Breathe it.

Don't blanket email large groups with a statement of disciplinary actions that's meant for one individual. Go to the source, put on your red high-heels, and take care of it, face-to-face.

Remember: Great leaders empower leaders.

Discover the strengths and passions of those you work with. Help others play to their strengths.

Don't create a team, survey, or ask for feedback if your mind is already made up.

Likewise, don't call meetings if it can be written in an email.

Making mistakes is OK. Say, "I'm sorry."

Share your passions and your quirks, overtly. Why not? We are all a little odd.

Bring your fidgets to admin meetings. It's OK for them to see adults have needs, too.

You will get LOTS of help along the way. Take time to thank them for saving you hours, and sometimes YEARS, of troubleshooting. Then, pay it forward.

Share even if no one notices your work.

 Wear ONE face—that one you see in the mirror!

Provide on-demand support.

Keep your door open and your phone nearby.

Respond to those in need even if you don't have the answer. It's perfectly OK to say, "I don't know, but I'll get back to you as soon as I find out."

A little feedback goes a long way.

Don't forget to acknowledge those that DO the work.

Great leaders are, often, invisible glue.

Tara, schedule protected time to ensure teaching never becomes foreign. This is your purpose in this life!

Make it a priority to learn from students.

Stay curious and full of wonder.

Be instrumental in building a positive culture.

Stay connected to your PLN.

Be strong. Be bold. Smile.

Keep the kids at the CENTER of all you do!

Flex in the mirror every once in a while.

Be REAL.

Love,

#TheRookieAdmin

Part 4

Learning Through Life

"I've had an exceptionally rare teacher who shifted my world on its axis. Sure, they taught me about the given subject but more than that they taught me always to be kind. They emphasized mental health and communication. They showed me that it was okay to be imperfect and that being right is not necessarily everything."

—Rachel, twelfth grade, Texas

Most people would describe me as a curious creature—an energized curious creature might be a bit more accurate. When I took the Gallup StrengthsFinder survey, it was no surprise that my number one strength was learner.

Learning is so ingrained in my DNA that I can barely relax and enjoy downtime. I often feel as if I should be learning something, reading a book, watching an instructional YouTube video, creating something—anything but just sitting and chilling out. I view life as a great, big learning opportunity.

As I considered what it means to be REAL, I knew the *L* would have something to do with learning.

A while back, I was chatting with my friend Nick Davis about how he gamifies his classroom. One statement he made lodged in my heart and mind: "You don't have to know the end to begin. That's the amazing part about it. You're the game designer." For a couple of weeks, Nick's words played over and over in my mind like my favorite song on repeat. (I even wrote a poem about it.) The more I thought about it, the more I realized that is Learning through Life!

What we learn through life keeps us waking up and trying again the next day.

Life is an adventure. We know not the end.

Sometimes we power up.

Sometimes we're knocked down.

Sometimes we're knocked out.

No matter the quest, an innovator's inner explorer can't stop; it won't settle. The twists and turns keep us guessing and striving for the next step.

My mind marvels at the mysteriousness of life. Just when you think you have an idea for how a series of events might go, something new and different interrupts your well-laid plan. Many times, this interruption leads to a more beautiful adventure. But there are times when everything comes to an abrupt stop—a dead end. So, while we may not know the end of this thing called life, until we reach the final end, we can always turn around or take a new path.

Life is ever changing. It's multifaceted and unpredictable. But one thing we all share in common is each of us has the choice to learn through life.

Throughout this section of the book, I will share a few learning through life experiences. Many times, there were no real plans, no standards to master, or rubrics to follow; just one choice that led to many others, an idea that led to more ideas, a question that bred more questions. With each new venture, however, I hope to grow, learn, and inspire others to be REAL. By sharing these personal encounters, I hope to inspire you to do the same with those within your realm of influence.

When we share our learning through life experiences, others will indeed learn new things in the process that might help them along life's journey. Unfortunately, there is little transparency regarding the learning process. Those are the moments omitted on social media in favor of the final product, with all its beauty displayed for all the world to see. The final product isn't the REAL story. Let's bind together and break down the barriers of this facade and share the L in REAL—Learning through Life. Inspiration can be found along the journey.

Heart-Healthy Salt

13

A couple of years ago, Simon Sinek's book, *Start with Why*, changed my life. Sinek's book taught me it is imperative to uncover and understand our life's true purpose—our why. Our purpose, he explains, should guide every move we make.

When we understand our why, we have a filter through which to sift our ideas to help us determine our next moves—the choices we make along life's journey. When we go through life without understanding our purpose, we will likely devote precious time to things that lead us astray from our goal or what we were meant to do.

After applying Sinek's *Start with Why* principles to my own life, I began to carefully observe people who had gained my admiration and who I considered influential. I listened intently as they discussed what made them feel successful in life. Each person measures success differently, so I looked for a few specific things in their unique definitions:

- Do those I consider influential know their why?
- Are they enjoying the journey of learning through life?
- Do they filter their actions through their purpose?
- Do they do what they love and love what they do?
- Do they influence others to strive for greatness?

It was easy to spot those who did, indeed, know their why. They did not focus on money or material things, rather they measured success by their enjoyment of work. In the process of learning through life, they sought to make a difference in others' lives. Some of them did manage to gain financial wealth for their sacrifices of time and energy, but one thing remained consistently true of those that knew their why: they were driven to crush goals and encourage others to do the same.

They could not anticipate every twist and turn along life's journey, but they enjoyed the ride anyway. They traveled through life with purpose and certainty. Their contagious confidence captivated me and caused me to desire more of what they had.

What Is Your *Why?*

My why is my purpose: Be REAL.

Relatable

Being relatable means embracing an amateur's spirit. I know that regardless of where I am on my journey, there is something meaningful to learn from others. Being relatable is also about sharing reflections and showing empathy, which helps me to build valuable relationships.

Expose Vulnerability

Criticism is a distinct possibility when exposing vulnerability, but each experience remains a learning opportunity. There are parts of my life I will never reveal publicly, but sharing some raw spots and allowing others to see my REAL humanity is of great value. It helps others recognize that we are all on a constant journey of improvement and are all on a different waypoint along that journey.

Approachable

Being approachable and sharing ideas that are applicable is what I strive to attain. Few things are more exciting than meeting someone you view as an influential icon in your life and realizing they are completely REAL. The pedestal you have placed them upon has not diminished their ability to be reached. I believe status should never taint a person's REALness and approachability.

Learning Through Life

How many times have you learned from someone else's mistakes? Time and experience are incredible teachers, but learning from someone else's experiences can save you so much heartache!

Sharing the lessons you've learned just might save someone else the heartache you've had to overcome. And the act of sharing those lessons is a powerful tool for building trust and fostering sustainable relationships. Most people want to know they are not alone and are willing to learn from the mistakes of others.

Being REAL is my purpose. It's the way I encourage and inspire people as they reach for their why.

Make Others Thirsty for Your Why

You've probably heard the proverb, "You can lead a horse to water, but you can't make it drink." But you may not have heard the second portion of that ancient wisdom: "but you can salt the hay."

How do you salt the hay and make others thirsty to discover their why but also inspired to learn more about your why?

The following section of *Start with Why* led me to discover the salt. Sinek explains,

Manipulation and inspiration both tickle the limbic brain. Aspirational messages, fear, or peer pressure all push us to decide one way or another by appealing to our irrational desires or playing on our fears. But it's when that emotional feeling goes deeper than insecurity or uncertainty or dreams that the emotional reaction aligns with how we view ourselves. It is at that point that behavior moves from being motivated to inspired. When we are inspired, the decisions we make have more to do with who we are and less to do with the companies or products we're buying.

Inspiration is the heart-healthy salt that flavors our why. Dr. Martin Luther King Jr. was a master at inspiring people with his passionate speeches and actions of devotion. He did not allow opposition to stop him from sharing his dream, his purpose, his why. Neither did he manipulate people or demand that others believe his message. He inspired them! He seasoned the nation with his passion for equality in hopes of making people thirsty enough to move toward that objective.

Heart-Healthy Salt

What makes heart-healthy salt different from your why? Heart-healthy salt is your what—the actions you take to influence others to thirst after the why.

Inspiration is the
heart-healthy
salt that
flavors our why.

Your whats can come from a variety of influences or life experiences. For example, your whats might evolve from your passions, or maybe they are discovered from a cannonball in idea? And, there are times your whats are formed from your life experiences.

Life Experience Salt

I have a cousin who is deaf, and at an early age, I learned limited American Sign Language so I could communicate with her. (Granted she was brilliant at reading lips, but I learned ASL.) As a child, I was completely fascinated with the language and how the words came alive when signing. This desire only increased as I entered adulthood.

In undergraduate school, I took a few American Sign Language courses, because I wanted to incorporate ASL in my classroom. As a teacher, I taught students the signs for requesting to go to the restroom, taking a break, moving from one thing to the next, counting, learning new vocabulary words, and even simple gestures of gratitude and celebrations. The students loved sharing their knowledge with their peers on the playground, and I loved the fact that these transition conversations were less disturbing during direct instruction. Students could inform me they were going to the restroom while I was teaching a small group math lesson, and I could answer in ASL without anyone missing a beat.

I also have a love for music. I play the piano and enjoy incorporating music in just about anything I do. ASL provided us an outlet to infuse music in the classroom, too. It sounds strange, but each year we would learn several songs in sign language and perform them for the visitors who came to our school on Veterans Day. The soldiers loved it as we signed songs such as "The Star Spangled Banner," "Hero" by Mariah Carey, and many other patriotic songs.

Signing songs made the words come alive. We even signed songs to help us learn academic content. But more than merely entertaining, ASL helped us not only learn a new language but also gain the deeper meaning of the words. By tapping into multiple senses to anchor the knowledge, we increased our content memory retention.

ASL is a what to reach my why; it is heart-healthy salt that makes words (and learning) come alive. It all began with the need to communicate with my little cousin as a child, but it later became a desired approach to help season the world. Sometimes life experiences create heart-healthy salt. This situation is unique to me, but what life experiences do you use to season those within your realm of influence?

If you're interested in infusing ASL in your classroom, there are several videos online to learn basic phrases that fit into the classroom setting.

Passion Salt

Heart-healthy salt can also be formed by incorporating a personal passion to solve a problem. As a third-grade teacher, I noticed that a significant number of our intermediate students (grades three through five) were struggling with reading fluency and comprehension. It was so evident that we had a schoolwide goal to help raise our students' reading achievement scores.

After school hours, I noticed a lot of our students would hang out at the park next door; many times, they were still there when I left work at least two hours after school had dismissed.

It hit me one day: What would the students think of a drama club? I conducted a survey to see what they thought of the idea. Enough interest was expressed, so I found a website (badwolfpress.com) that offered scripts of musical productions at all grade levels and aligned with the national standards. We didn't always sing the songs, but I loved music, and the rhyme was helpful for struggling readers. . The students did not have to pay to attend, but they had to show interest by signing up—not their parents signing them up. It was interest-based. It seemed like a dream come true; we could not only provide the kids with something meaningful to do after school, but I could also monitor improvement of comprehension and fluency of the students with reading deficiencies.

The students loved the idea, and we began putting on a winter and a spring show. I enjoyed integrating my love of music and acting into the learning environment, and while it was time consuming and challenging at times, the sacrifice was well worth the results. The drama club cast discovered confidence when playing to their passions of acting; it was a wonderful experience for all of us—the kids, the parents, their classroom teachers, and me. The lessons we learned proved valuable not only for reading, but for life; and I imagine they will never forget our after-school rehearsal fun—which usually started and ended with short dance parties. We loved celebrating our learning, and our state assessment scores proved that learning while having fun can improve reading comprehension and fluency.

Incorporating music and acting into learning environments is another way I sprinkle heart-healthy salt upon those within my realm of influence. What is your flavor of engagement? What is your passion salt?

Too Much Salt

I love sharing my learning but there are times others might find my enthusiasm a bit too salty. I have found that educators just do not have as much time as they would like to spend taking in content or new learning. They would love to, but their lives are simply consumed. With learner as my number one Gallup Strength, another what to flavor the world, I always make time to learn something new.

Therefore, as an administrator, I decided to get creative about bringing the learning opportunities to those I serve.

A Dash of Salt

#PottyPD is simple way to bring the learning to your staff or colleagues. Have you recently read a blog or book that you'd love to share a highlight? Or , do you create newsletters that it seems as though no one takes the time to read? Make a few bullet points, add color, a few images, and print enough to post on the backs of the stalls in the staff restroom or above the urinals. Everyone has to take a break at some point; provide them some #PottyPD for learning on the go. Restroom salt? Yes, indeed.

#3minPD is a short YouTube video series that I began to share learning reflections for those that don't want to read but would rather listen in the car or watch as they are walking the treadmill. These quick reflection blurbs have been utilized by my principal friends in staff meetings and among the coaches when leading professional development discussions. If you'd like to explore more #3minPD video clips, check out the resource tab below. However, I'd encourage you to create some, as well; let's learn through life together——three minutes at a time.

There are so many whats to help us reach our why, but you have to discover what works well for you. Be it a life experience salt that teaches you a desired approach to reach your why or a passion salt that is unique to you, everyone has heart-healthy salt; we must use it to learn through life.

Why?

Your why has to be much bigger than your what. Your why is the purpose that encompasses all areas of life. When talking to educators and friends about their whys, I have noticed many consider their whats as their whys.

If your why and what seem difficult to differentiate, zoom way out and consider your REAL and unique purpose. You why is something others can attain or have a part in. It is something artificial intelligence or technology cannot replicate. It is REAL and, once discovered, truly puts everything else in perspective.

My why is being REAL in all areas of life and encouraging others to do the same. My whats are writing, speaking, coaching, hugging those in need, mentoring my son, sharing my heart via blogs and vlogs, caring for my family, inspiring educators and friends globally, etc. My whats are fueled by my passion—my motivation. That's how I will reach my why.

People often ask me, "Tara, where do you get your inspiration? Your energy? What makes you an overcomer?

My inspiration comes from my why—deep within. It's being REAL to the core. In fact, I try to measure every decision I make using two questions:

How will this action help me achieve my purpose—my why?

What positive impact will it have on the people I serve?

Season the World

In what ways do your whats not only lead others to thirst for your why but also cause them to seek and discover their unique contribution to the whole process?

Are you doing what you can do to influence as many people as possible to thirst after your why? If you hide your salt, others will never taste it. But if we are intentional about our whats, others will thirst for our why while seeking to discover their own why. They will want more of what you have.

Dr. Martin Luther King Jr. influenced generations of people to share his dream through his powerful speeches—his whats—and millions joined with him to help fulfill his why. By sharing your whats, you will begin to build a community around your why, and your message will spread and quench the thirst of many.

Recognize your talents and strengths and own them! Then, make confident choices. Take the leap and try out an idea, teach, lead, write, speak, encourage a friend over coffee—do what you do and begin to salt the world with your whats. Don't doubt yourself. That may be easier said than done, but if an idea, action, or next step fits your purpose—your why—go with it!

- What is your why?
- Keep in mind, your why should transcend your current role. If it is limited to one role, it is most likely heart-healthy salt that leads to your why. Zoom out and think big.
- What is your heart-healthy salt? How do you season the world and make others thirsty to share your why?

Please share your reflections using the #REALedu hashtag, and visit tarammartin.com/bereal for more Chapter 13 heart-healthy exercises.

The Beauty of Blogging

14

Writing has been a passion of mine for many years.

It all began when I was about eight years old. My second-grade teacher bought me a tiny little diary and said, "You can share your thoughts here. You can lock it up, keep the key, and store your journal in the bottom drawer of my file cabinet. You may share your writing with me, but if you choose not to, I'll not peek inside."

As I would write, I noticed I felt light inside and worried less about not having everything under control.

Thirty-one years later, writing took a new turn for me when I began my website.

I rarely had, if ever, shared my writing with others. Writing was my best friend. It held my hand through so many adventures in life. It hugged me when I was scared. It never left me and was always there when I needed it. Now we were to be exposed to the world. Would that change our bond? Could we do that? Could we share our REAL with the world?

Fear gripped me as I considered those questions, but I reminded myself that I don't write for accolades or fame.

I write because it makes me feel alive. It's a *what* to my *why*. No matter the mood or tone of the words on the page, the activity fills my heart with delight and with a sense of closure. Writing is my voice when I can't speak. It's the way I share my voice with the world.

When I write, I feel a sense of accomplishment. Not because it needs approval from others, but because I managed to snag a few racing thoughts within my wild imagination and connect them to something REAL while creating something meaningful.

Writing makes me feel complete; it's therapeutic. Like a wildfire trapped inside my chest begging to escape, I cannot contain my words, so I allow them to burst free and burn vividly on the page. Writing is my mouthpiece. It's the heart-healthy salt I sprinkle in the world. It's my energy, my thought collector, and the calm to my crazy.

This heart-healthy salt provides me an outlet to expose my innermost being—which feels scary, yet restorative. It's my time capsule, my personal history book; it helps me learn from my past, present, and dream big for the future.

I write because it sustains life in my heart, soul, and mind. It's one of many shakes from my personal heart-healthy salt shaker to season the earth with my *why*—my REAL purpose.

Clearly, writing is a prominent piece of the REAL me, but when I met George Couros in that parking lot at iPadpalooza, I told him I wanted to start my own website and maybe a blog. Maybe blog? I had been writing for years. For what was I waiting? He was super blunt in asking why I had not done so already—why was I still thinking about it? I had no excuses. Long story short, he helped me get my website set up, and so began a journey that has birthed endless opportunities. In fact, my blog became salt to share my REAL message far and wide.

Even though I journaled daily for years, when I started my blog, I worried and wondered if others would even want to read it. With a little encouragement from my PLN, I began using my website as a professional digital portfolio, which is how George had encouraged me to set it up.

The framework of the blog was key for me. Once I understood that the purpose of reflecting through a professional portfolio was to capture my learning through life moments, I desired to organize it in a way that would best serve those within my realm of influence.

The Blogging Framework

About Me—This section contains a little information about me for others to peek in and see who I am and what I value, both professionally and personally.

Why REAL?—I wanted others to know my *why* and publicly wanted to share my filter for measuring future posts. It was more of an accountability piece for me.

Professional Standards—George taught me this piece. I made a specific tab for the standards for which I was evaluated. These standards became categories for tagging. If a leadership standard could not be tagged, the blog post might not belong on my professional portfolio.

I later added these components:

Resources—As I would create resources to contribute to my PLN or within my blog, I began saving links to them within this section.

REAL Feedback—In this section, I embedded Tweets that mentioned me inspiring or encouraging others via my blog, in a workshop, keynote, or just in conversation. This has been a very encouraging reflection piece of the portfolio for me. It took me a little while to build a PLFamily. So this tab did not appear on my website until a while later.

Keynotes and Presentations—At first, I had only spoken at our district conference. Therefore, I began creating a list of workshops and presentations I gave and listed the dates beside each one. This section later evolved to where it is now.

I believe every educator should begin their own professional, digital portfolio. I encourage you to create and maintain your own journey of blogging and reflecting on your professional practice. Your framework might look different, and that's OK. By modeling my learning journey, I have encouraged the educators I serve to create their own websites. Many of the instructional coaches I lead, as well as the educators I serve, have now created a professional digital portfolio, and each of their sites look different and unique; but one thing remains consistent—they are now sharing their learning through life moments with the world. In fact, several of the coaches now teach "How to Create a Professional Digital Portfolio" and "Find Meaning in Sharing Your Learning Journey" (sessions I once taught) in local and state conferences. Side note: I don't even teach those sessions in my district any longer; the teachers and coaches take the lead. Cannonball in! It's worth it. You have nothing to lose and many things to gain by blogging.

Professional Time Capsule

Writing is how I reflect. It is a way of connecting my thoughts and making sense of them before I react. However, now my reflections can be reflected upon by others—and that was a scary thought. At first, knowing others could read my blog intimidated me. I didn't want to write my true feelings for fear of what my readers might think. But if

I were to fulfill the purpose of my website and be REAL, I had to be honest—professional, but honest.

This honesty came to life when I decided my blog was a place to document professional growth. After all, that was its purpose; it was created to be a Professional Digital Portfolio. As soon as I shifted my mindset, it stopped taking me forty-seven revisions to press Publish. I no longer worried, What if (name any educational icon here) reads this? I even stopped wondering, What if no one reads this? Because even if no one read it, I used the platform to serve a purpose. It held my professional "current reality" so one day I could look back and see growth over time.

I love going back and reading posts from a year ago. I cannot wait until I have spent five, ten, twenty years blogging. What growth will I be able to see in one central location? Heck, I had to change my About Me and update my resume two times in one year because it became inaccurate.

A website is always a work in progress, but that is the beauty of capturing the growth and journey in this professional time capsule. It is a personal history book. When you think about blogging like that, it doesn't seem so scary at all. You're competing with no one, you're just documenting your journey.

It Goes Before You

When applying for administrator positions, my website was at the top of my resume. (See visual representation of my resume in the Monitor Your Heart section of this chapter.) I really had no idea if the interview teams would view it when selecting candidates, but it was now a curation of my professional journey—well, a year of it anyway. Side note: I wish I had started this blogging journey my first year of teaching; what a beautiful way to share growth.

When sitting in those interviews, it was always a nice surprise when the committee members would say things like, "We saw _____ on your website. Tell us more about how you encourage educators to embrace this strategy." They asked me about #BookSnaps, because they saw Tweets from several students using #BookSnaps around the country in the REAL Feedback section. They inquired about presentations I had given. And rather than struggling to provide unique answers to typical interview questions, my answers to these questions rolled off my tongue from a place deep within—a place of pure passion that I had explored, documented, and reflected upon. Granted, there were a few of the traditional questions that caused me to pause and ponder my next word, but, for the most part, the whole process felt more like a conversation. It's likely that topics mentioned in those interviews would have never come up had I been answering a slew of canned questions.

Needless to say, I did not land all three of the positions I interviewed for, but each of the committees knew who I was—even before I arrived for the first face-to-face encounter. I did land the position that wanted what I had to offer. I was selected for the district administrator position because my blog served its purpose. It was the heart-healthy salt that caused the interviewing committee to thirst for more of the REAL me.

Technology cannot replace authentic human beings, but it is a tool to share and amplify your REAL self with the world. How else might one share (in detail) their professional journey during a thirty- to forty-five-minute interview?

Think about educator websites from the interviewing committee's perspective. If a candidate has a website with video clips of their

Technology cannot replace authentic human beings, but it is a tool to share and amplify your REAL self with the world.

performance, REAL feedback from others around the world, and blog posts revealing reflections of professional practices—the good, the bad, and the ugly—how might that compare to a two-page resume of other candidates? Granted, maybe after learning so much about the candidate, they could decide the person is not the perfect fit. But that's a blessing in disguise, if you ask me. Wouldn't you want the job where your REAL self fits in like the perfect puzzle piece?

Let your website go before you. Do not be afraid. Just salt the world. Let them taste and see if your REAL fits their liking, and if it does not, find that place where you can thrive and fulfill your purpose—your *why*.

A REAL Clone

Every year I send out a performance survey to gauge the teachers' perceptions of my service. I serve more than three-hundred educators, and it is difficult to know exactly how they perceive my performance unless I ask. I have done some type of perception survey since I was a classroom teacher because I have yet to master reading minds.

I always find the results of these surveys incredibly meaningful and sometimes humorous. I take what I learn and use it to grow. I fix what I can, and sometimes I just have to let things go. Since this is a perception survey, the educators share their point of view; for example, "I could see through your dress during our last district-wide PD." Yes, that is one easily fixed. Check! Never will I wear that dress again. However, those things that are out of my control to fix or find resources for, such as, "She smiles too much," I merely dismiss. You never know what you might get, and that is the beauty of tapping into the minds of those you serve.

While analyzing the feedback my first year as a district administrator, I noticed many comments from teachers and principals referring to my blog. At first, I was baffled they even knew I had a blog. Sure, it is on the signature line of my email, but I never asked anyone to follow it. Their feedback implied they knew me. It was as if I had built a REAL relationship with more than one-hundred educators (a third of those I serve, who responded). I hadn't visited with all of them face-to-face very many times. But they knew me and my *why* based on my posts. They even utilized resources I had placed on my website and would comment how these strategies were impacting the learning of their students and staff members.

My blog is my clone. That might sound silly, but I was able to be in classrooms and impact hundreds of teachers and students when, physically, that would be impossible. If that was happening in my district, what about those who subscribed to my website around the world?

If you can't physically travel the world, you can certainly get there by blogging. Being transparent, relevant, exposing a little vulnerability, and sharing my learning through life experiences has opened doors for me locally, nationally, and globally. The professional learning opportunities that have been birthed have and continue to allow me to season the world with more heart-healthy salt.

Be it speaking gigs, writing opportunities, or arranging meetings to network face-to-face with educators, students, and friends around the world, many doors have swung wide open and have allowed me to share my REAL self with others through my professional digital portfolio. There is no doubt many people would never know the *why* from this girl in Kansas had my website not been a part of my journey.

It's a no-brainer: If you want to spread your salt far and wide and allow others to try it and see if it fits their tastes, but have yet to clone yourself, begin a professional digital portfolio. It might be too salty for some, but it could be the exact seasoning needed for others. You'll never know until you hit Publish.

Cannonball in!

Transparency Empowers

One of the reasons I blog is because doing so provides an outlet for me to pay it forward by sharing ideas, influences, lessons learned, and exposing a little vulnerability, while encouraging others to maximize their REAL potential as well. I moved from being a consumer only to being a contributor, and that was a game changer for my career. My website and passion for writing truly became heart-healthy salt that seasoned an authentic, global audience.

What is your *why*—your purpose—your story?

What is that thing you love, your fire within, your passion?

Are you sharing your passions to achieve your purpose and salt the world with your *why*? Or are you afraid to expose your *whats* with the world?

Modeling the learning process openly and publicly through your website is a beautiful example of being REAL. Think about it. How might being transparent with your learning through life moments empower those you serve? Your why is every bit a part of you! In fact, you might try but you can't contain this wildfire within, nor will you escape it.

Our educational system needs others to expose a little vulnerability and create that healthy blood flow to sustain our edu-heart. Yes, we can do this within our district or school, but why not break though geographical boundaries and shake that heart-healthy salt all over the world?

Blogging and maintaining a website is a continual work in progress. And it's that learning through the process that makes blogging such an excellent example for those you serve. We must continue to do our part, day in and day out. I love this quote from Rory Vaden: "Success is never owned; it's rented. And rent is due every day."

So do your part and encourage everyone around you to do theirs. When the critics taunt you, remember your why! Consider the question, "Is this heart-healthy salt to cause others to thirst for my why?" If the answer is yes—do it.

Don't let fear stop you. Let's learn through life together!

- In what ways do you openly share your professional reflections?
- What section would you add to the framework above? Why?
- How might a digital professional portfolio benefit you and those you serve?

Please share your reflections using the #REALedu hashtag, and visit tarammartin.com/bereal for more Chapter 14 heart-healthy exercises.

Cannonball into #BookSnaps

15

In August 2016, every time saw my son, Kaleb, he was snapping pictures and sending them to dozens of friends. His life, it seemed to me, was a constant stream of selfies and short bursts of text to communicate with his friends all over the world in an app called Snapchat.

That month, when I viewed the usage analytics of our cell phone bill, I had to rub my eyes and check it twice. For an average of seven hours a day, my child was on Snapchat! I flipped out when I showed this data to my husband. I told my husband he had to remove the app. There is no way in the world anyone should spend that much time sending selfies. He must be on the app all day long. How is he making straight A's in school?

I tried hard to imagine the benefits of being that connected to his friends. No matter what I considered, I still felt frustrated.

Why was I irritated? Were his actions harming his performance in school? No. He still talked and interacted with those he was around. He still talked to us. He even snapped pics of us to send to his friends. (I'm not 100 percent sure I liked that idea, either.)

For some reason, I could not handle the idea of him spending that much time on Snapchat. I didn't have any hard evidence as to whether or why it was a problem, but in my mind, I leaned toward the idea that he needed more social interaction. He needs face-to-face time with people, thus all the selfies. Fed up with all the snapping, one day I said, "Kaleb, why do you insist on spending so much time on Snapchat? I'm considering removing the app from your phone. You spend far too many hours during a day on that app."

"Mom, you don't understand," he replied. "This is how kids communicate with each other. If I don't have Snapchat, I wouldn't be able to talk to my friends every day, those locally and back home in Texas. This is how we talk to each other! We use snaps (pictures) to share how we are feeling and tell each other about our day. Why would you take that away from me? How did you talk to your friends when you were my age?"

I listened, working hard to understand his point of view. This was how he connected with his friends. My husband and I reflected on the hours and hours we spent talking on the phone, with the cord stretched across the house so we could hide in the washroom for privacy. We also recalled endless pager messages that were typed in code to let the other know we were thinking of them. After considering the ridiculous number of hours we spent communicating with our friends via the limited technology we had as teens, we decided to allow him to keep the app on his phone.

All that snapping still drove me bonkers, but we let it go.

The Solution

Well, let's be honest. I tried to let it go. About a week later, I decided to do what I coach teachers to do all the time: diligently work to find a way to use Snapchat for edu-awesomeness. But how?

I had seen teachers using Snapchat video reflections and posting them on Twitter, but I was searching for something unique. As I sat down to read that evening, I steadily highlighted sections in my book and made annotations in the margins. On this particular day, I had drawn a few icons to remember the content in that section of my book. That is when the idea hit me.

I called Kaleb down from upstairs, "Kaleb, come teach mom how to use Snapchat! I have an idea I'd like to try."

He came downstairs and gave me a *What?! Nooooo . . . you're old!* look but agreed to help me. After all, this might be his gateway to me not badgering him about his favorite social media app. I began to tell him how I'd like to snap a picture of the page in my book, use the text feature to annotate the quote and my key takeaways, and then recreate the imagery in my mind with emojis and Bitmojis.

To which he responded, "Mom, you're an ultimate nerd!"

But he taught me how to do just that. He walked me through the non-intuitive app and showed me, in detail, how to accomplish my goal. He even helped me create my own Bitmoji. And when I snapped my first pic, it was just what I had imagined: a digital, visual representation of everything I had handwritten in the margins of my book. Now, I wanted to share it with anyone and everyone, but how?

What better place to share it but my newly discovered global platform: Twitter. I wrote my Tweet, attached my image, tagged the author and publisher of the book, Dave Burgess, and gave it a name—#BookSnaps.

Done.

I hadn't spent hours thinking about it. I just did it. I posted my first #BookSnaps image on Twitter within minutes of having the idea, and I didn't consider how the world (okay, my fifty-ish followers on Twitter at that time) might react to it. In other words, I had no notion or expectation even of the kind of splash or the ripple effect #BookSnaps might have. I just cannonballed in because I wanted to share what I was learning—and maybe find a way to connect students to learning, using technology they apparently loved.

Learning by Doing

That same month, I was hosting a book study with the novice instructional coaches I was mentoring. I shared this idea of #BookSnaps with them, and they agreed that between our scheduled meetings, we would create #BookSnaps of the book *Launch* by A.J. Juliani and John Spencer. Each time I'd create #BookSnaps, I'd Tweet them out and tag the authors, the publisher, and hashtag the book title.

One day, Dave Burgess, author of *Teach Like a PIRATE*, commented on the #BookSnaps. He loved them! I mentioned earlier how excited I was to virtually meet one of my edu-heroes on Twitter. While replying to his Tweet, I had to keep reminding myself to be calm and cool. *Remember*, I told myself, *he is a REAL person—and he is complimenting your work!* I remained calm and professional on Twitter. (Thank goodness he couldn't see my giddy expression as I typed!) I thanked him for the compliment and immediately made a few more #BookSnaps. That's what behavior-specific praise does!

Share with the World

Later, I wrote a blog about this crazy idea and titled it "#BookSnaps—Snapping for Learning." In it, I told the story about how Kaleb was driving me bonkers on Snapchat and how that ulti-mately led to the birth of #BookSnaps. I talked about how I cannon-balled in and tried it during my book study with the instructional coaches I mentored.

I also shared that, although #BookSnaps started with adult learn-ers, I planned to keep student learning the key motivator. The ques-tions I reflected on in my original #BookSnaps blog still make my heart smile.

1. How might we find ways for students to use this method for reflecting on the content they are learning?

2. Will speaking their Snapchat language encourage more interaction with the book, content, or topic?

3. How might students share #BookSnaps with teachers via other platforms—Google Classroom, SeeSaw, Twitter class-room, etc.

I created a how-to video for creating #BookSnaps and posted it on YouTube, added the link and a few images to the post—then revised the blog fifty-two times—and hit Publish! Yes, you read that correctly: fifty-two revisions. I still giggle at how many times I used to revise my posts in the beginning stages of my blog.

If you're not familiar with #BookSnaps or Snapchat and are won-dering how it works, trust me; you're in safe hands. I have been trained by the Master Snapchatter, Mr. Kaleb Martin, aka my then fifteen-year-old, not-so-little-man! You can see the original post and video at tarammartin.com/booksnaps-snapping-for-learning, but here are the instructions in a nutshell:

1. Download Snapchat from Google Play or the App Store.

2. Add your book study pals by clicking the little ghost and "Add Friends by Username."

3. Begin documenting your reflections as you read.

A few (of many) reasons to create #BookSnaps:

- Annotate and share excerpts of the book you're reading
- Allows the reader to connect an idea or thought by creating a digital visual representation (The visual representation solidifies the text content within the mind and signals the brain to retrieve the idea from memory.)
- Diagram the rise, fall, and climax of the plot (see an example image below)
- Highlight figurative language and imagery
- Notate character conflict and internal struggles (see example below)
- To personally connect to the text—this is my favorite!
- Point out the main idea or a supporting argument
- Has its own hashtag on Twitter: #BookSnaps!
- It's easy! Just read, snap, reflect, add stickers, share, and repeat.

Okay, are you ready? Cannonball!

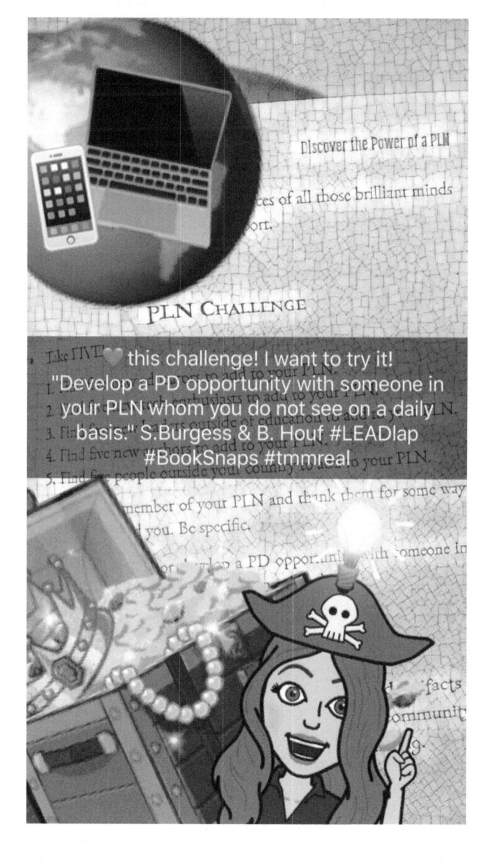

The kids still laughed, now more hysterically than ever, as Cameron got up from under the bench. He felt more and more anger pulsing through his frail body. Only the wasp distracted Cameron from going nuts on the entire team. He felt like a man who wanted revenge and a home run would prove that he could be just like the other boys. *I'll show them.*

Cameron grabbed a bat and headed straight for the batter's box. Instead of looking at the ground, he held his head high. He glared at the boys lined up behind the backstop. Richie Dunford was ready to pitch, but he couldn't stop laughing at Cameron. Even though the boys were playing underhand softball, Richie was known for his wicked pitching arm. He could throw a softball like a cannonball coming out of a four-barrel, twenty-millimeter, anti-aircraft, World War II, cannon.

Cameron gripped the bat as tightly as he could, clenched his teeth, and whispered under his breath,

👀 at the simile-> "He could throw a softball like a cannonball coming out of a four-barrel, twenty millimeter, anti-aircraft, World War II, cannon." Rick Jetter & The Isolate /n./

"Strike one!" yelled Mr. Elton. The whole baseball diamond laughed. So did the trees as they rustled

Richie fired another pitch. Cameron swung the bat, as he could, but couldn't even hit the ball around the ball.

"Strike two!" yelled Mr. Elton. The laughter grew louder.

"C'mon, Richie, I know your game now," Cameron said. He clenched the bat as if he hit a burglar trying to mug an old lady in an alley. He felt like he was outside of his into a hailstorm of fireballs, flames and his *enemies*

Richie looked around at his fellow comrades, still laughing. Everyone

Richie stared at Cameron with a and, no person tred. It was super easy for Richie to too. Cameron had never done when Richie grew for Richie.

Stick with Your *Why*

Within a month of sharing this unique way to use technology to share the learner's thinking with the world, an educator, who has been very influential in my life, contacted me and said, "What is this #BookSnaps thing?"

I excitedly explained my fresh idea to him and how it was completely underdeveloped. I shared that I wanted to find an educational use for the app Snapchat and told him that the publisher of some of the books I'd featured liked it!

His response caught me off guard: "Tara, is this what you want to be known for? Is this your brand? I think you have more to offer than this #BookSnaps idea. Is that really all you have to offer?"

I was expecting him to say, "This sounds interesting, intriguing, has potential," anything of the sort. Instead the comment he shared threw me for a loop. I hadn't thought about #BookSnaps being my brand. I just cannonballed into an idea I found exciting. I hadn't even, at that time, considered any research behind the idea. It was just an idea that I had tossed into the Twittersphere.

I did not answer right away; I rarely do when I'm caught off guard. I've learned to think about my response before I speak. As I thought, I did what I usually do when considering whether something is worth the investment of my time and energy—I ran it through my why: Will #BookSnaps help students and/or adults be more REAL—relate to text or each other, expose a little vulnerability, find ways to approach their teacher or other readers with their ideas and learn through life?

The more I thought about, the more sure of myself I became. A day or so later, I answered my educator friend and said something like this:

"I don't know if #BookSnaps will be my brand. I hadn't even considered that thought. I do think it fits my brand—my purpose, my why. I think it will indeed be a type of heart-healthy salt to cause others to thirst after the REAL why."

He didn't push back much, just gave a bit more pointed advice and let me go on my merry way.

I think it's important to share this piece of my story. If we want others to thirst for our why, we must first know what it is. Then, we must use our why as a filter to determine how we will salt the world.

I could have felt the resistance from an established educator, a dear mentor, and stopped pursuing the development of #BookSnaps. It would have been easy to say, "Well, if he doesn't support it, maybe this isn't the best idea." But remember: Others' opinions do not determine our purpose. I chose to continue to develop the concept and get it into the hands of students to see how it might help them be REAL with the text they are reading and exploring. The feedback and results have been amazing, proving that sticking with my why was the right choice.

Don't let others persuade you to abandon heart-healthy salt. Salt the world with your why and make others thirsty for more.

Speaking of salt, #BookSnaps began to season the educational system on a global level when Dave Burgess asked me, in November of 2016, to write a guest post for his blog. Again, I'm so glad he couldn't hear the squeal of delight I made when I read his request. And then fear butted in: Me? I barely have my blog up and running and have maybe one or two subscribers—my husband being one. I assured Dave I didn't have enough experience with writing publicly and offered for him to write about #BookSnaps and feature the idea on his blog. He did not go for that. In his persistent Captain way, he insisted I write the post. He even said, "You can copy and paste what's on your blog. It's perfect—as is."

His comment sent me reeling again: THE Mr. Pirate has read my blog! And OM to the G, he wants me to write for his blog. This is really happening!

I was honored and, clearly, a bit starstruck. What could I do but agree to write the post, and on November 1, 2016, #BookSnaps began to salt the world—literally—and cause educators from all over the world to thirst for more. I'm forever grateful for Dave and the chance he took on my wild idea. Dave is the REAL deal; he motivates (and sometimes shoves) others to take risks and, in my terms, cannonball in! Because of Dave, educators all over the world began to flood my inbox with questions and reflections, and with each question, it fueled my fire to discover more depth to the #BookSnaps strategy.

monitor your heart rate

- In what ways do you integrate the passions of your students into learning?
- Describe a time you attempted to solve a problem and discovered a new (to you) strategy.
- Who helps amplify your voice and ideas? How do you amplify the voice and ideas of those you serve?
- How might you use #BookSnaps in your setting?
- Original Blog- #BookSnaps–Snapping for Learning
- **#BookSnaps How-To Videos**

Please share your reflections using the #REALedu hashtag, and visit tarammartin.com/bereal for more Chapter 15 heart-healthy exercises.

The Ripple Effect of #BookSnaps

16

The more questions that flooded my inbox, the more I realized I must discover some answers. I began comparing the #BookSnaps strategy with the reading comprehension neuroscience I had learned in undergraduate school. I remember reading about how the brain processes language in Marilyn Jager Adams' book, *Beginning to Read: Thinking and Learning about Print*. As I researched the brain processors used for reading and comprehending text, I found a few more current articles that confirmed my thoughts concerning how the reading brain works when all of the four processors in the left hemisphere of the brain are functioning properly. The best information I found to explain this process came from *LETRS® Module 1, 2nd Edition*, and it actually included Marilyn Jager Adams' research.

In short, it states how the brain has four processors that enable a student to learn to read and comprehend:

- The **phonological processor** helps us determine how sounds make words. This is the one we use when we first begin to learn to speak.

- The **orthographic processor** is used to help us determine how letters and sounds make written words.
- The **angler gurus** is a processor that works much like a mental file cabinet; it houses every word an individual knows, both verbal and printed vocabulary.
- The **context and meaning processor** helps us use words in context with the proper meaning.

When all these processors are firing as intended, the reader paints a visual image in their mind, commonly referred to as imagery or visualization.

So how does this relate to #BookSnaps? All of the brain activity described above occurs in the left hemisphere of the brain, but when a student recreates the imagery that has been developed within their mind in the form of a digital, visual representation, like #BookSnaps, they engage the right hemisphere of their brain—the creative artistic functionalities. With #BookSnaps, they are also using a language (in 2016, emojis and Bitmojis) they love and find relevant for communicating with their peers.

When both hemispheres of the brain are engaged, the chance of moving content from the working memory to the long-term memory increases exponentially. Therefore, if a student creates a #BookSnap at the beginning, middle, and end of the book, their chance of retaining the content around the areas where the BookSnap was created increases substantially. In many cases, #BookSnaps has improved reading comprehension.

It might sound strange, but after making #BookSnaps of the professional books I was reading, I was able to remember specific quotes, as well as the chapters in which the quotes could be found. I do not have a photographic memory, so this baffled me at first; however, the more I researched the reading comprehension neuroscience and the working memory science for engaging both hemispheres of the brain, the more this automatic recall of information made sense.

Students have demonstrated increased content memory retention with #BookSnaps as well. In fact, my son speaks about how #BookSnaps serve as an excellent study guide for his history class, where he would typically take notes or use an outline of study material. He claims that creating a visual representation and including the facts from the textbook in the form of #BookSnaps helps him better retain the material for the test—and long after the assessment.

One key piece my now-eleventh-grade son warns teachers about is not to make students upload their #BookSnaps to their Snap Story. This a story that is shared with their friends and uploading #BookSnaps is not ideal for teens. It's a social buzzkill!

Instead, have students save the #BookSnaps to their camera roll and upload them to a platform such as Padlet.com, Google Slides, Google Classroom, or any platform where they can curate images. This will also keep teachers from needing to friend their students on Snapchat. All of this information is explained in the how-to videos found in the link at the end of this chapter.

It's Not the App; It's the Science

Let me be clear: It's not the app; it's the science behind the strategy of visible thinking that makes this memory retention possible. It just so happens this strategy, #BookSnaps, is easily implemented with an app students love to use during this particular time frame.

Will #BookSnaps withstand the test of time? Yes. I have no idea what the future holds, or what interesting tech tool will be available in the coming months and years, but I know #BookSnaps will continue to be an effective learning strategy. If students have some way to share their learning through a digital, visual representation of their thoughts, they can create #BookSnaps.

Keep in mind, I did not know the science or effectiveness of #BookSnaps when I launched it into the EDUworld, but rather discovered them through action research—learning by doing.

I hope #BookSnaps serves to remind educators around the world that ideas need not be fully developed in order to test them for effectiveness. Sometimes, we are simply solving a problem (an I-don't-want-to-remove-the-app-from-my-teenage-son's-phone problem), and we happen to discover a valuable strategy that can be utilized to help students share their learning and thinking visibly, while increasing their learning retention of information.

Are you ready?

Cannonball in!

#BookSnaps Access for All

Once I discovered the science behind #BookSnaps, I wanted to ensure all students could utilize the strategy in some form—especially since I understood how it helps increase learning retention. Snapchat is an effective app for this use, but due to student age and school network restrictions, many were not able to access it.

I began experimenting with any app I could find that would allow one to edit an image, annotate with a text feature, and use stickers or emojis to create a visual representation of imagery. A few apps I discovered to be accessible to students of all ages around the world were Seesaw, Pic Collage, Book Creator, Buncee, Google Drawing, and Google Slides. #BookSnaps for everyone!

For more detailed instructions on how to create #BookSnaps with each of these apps, visit tarammartin.com/resources/booksnaps-how-to-videos.

#BookSnaps Cousins

After I wrote the guest blog for Dave Burgess and began sharing the science behind #BookSnaps, along with the many apps utilized to create them, the concept began to spread like wildfire.

Educators were connecting the idea to their relevant content and placing the word "snaps" behind it. I like to call these my #BookSnaps cousins.

For example: #sciencesnaps, #labsnaps, #mathsnaps, #writingsnaps, #FrenchSnaps, #SpanishSnaps, etc. There is even a culinary teacher in Oregon, Tisha Richmond, who used #foodsnaps for her students to share their thoughts after completing culinary projects.

#SuperBowlSnaps

One cousin that now sweeps the social media annually is the #SuperBowlSnaps. (I doubt this will appeal to my football fans out there, but hear me out. View these next few statements from the lens of a student who doesn't want to engage because the topic isn't of interest.) It was Super Bowl Sunday, and my Twitter buddy, Denis Sheeran, author of *Instant Relevance*, had this grand idea to create a cousin to #BookSnaps and call them #SuperBowlSnaps. I was a bit hesitant at first because I typically do not watch the Super Bowl. However, after seeing one of his examples, I cannonballed into the #SuperBowlSnaps pool.

For the first time, I was completely engaged in the game start to finish. My husband thought I was a bit nerdy, but, hey, what's new? I searched for learning opportunities, took snaps, and created a prompt for students and staff members to engage with the next day. Some snaps became writing prompts, while others were math challenges. I also created some snaps that were simply a conversation starter. Lesson planning in a snap!

They loved them! When we connect to students' (and adults') REAL interests, we make learning fun.

Everyone around knows you have it, yet in the heat of the struggle you can't see.
Share a time you had to PRESS through an obstacle to achieve success.
#SuperBowlSnaps #BookSnaps #tmmreal

#GratitudeSnaps

One of my favorite #BookSnaps cousins is #GratitudeSnaps. It began as a conversation between two good friends sharing the need to remain positive in the midst of all the would-be overwhelming negativity around us. I created a daily digital journal of the things for which I was grateful. Further heartfelt discussion with Tisha Richmond, culinary lead teacher in Oregon, led to a mission to storm social media with positivity via #GratitudeSnaps.

#GratitudeSnaps has indeed salted the world in a REAL way. Connected educators from around the world began sharing snaps of their families, their hobbies, and passions, the little things they value in everyday activities. With each snap, I began to see a more rounded, REAL, person on the other end of the computer screen, and my face and heart smile at how much we are alike—and how many diverse talents, passions, and values we bring to the world of education.

How might #GratitudeSnaps help to create a positive culture in your class, school, or school district? See the resource tab at the conclusion of this chapter for more information on #GratitudeSnaps.

Cannonball in! Make a splash and share the ripple effects!

Day 9 #GratitudeSnaps - Thankful for my little Best Friend and Rootbeer Floats! She can count on me to introduce her to the finer things in life! She 🖤'd it! #tmmreal

#REALyouSnaps

The most recent cousin of #BookSnaps is the #REALyouSnaps. I recently read a book via global read aloud to a group of first graders in Florida in Brandi Miller's class (@bmilla84 on Twitter). We read *Exclamation Mark* by Amy Krouse Rosenthal and Tom Lichtenheld. After reading this book, I challenged the students to create a snap using the app Seesaw to share what makes them unique and REAL, and we called these snaps #REALyouSnaps. The results were astounding. Take a peek at a few examples below.

Brandi's Reflections on the #REALyouSnaps

> *#REALyouSnaps provided my students with a unique opportunity to showcase what makes them special. They had creative freedom as they designed a digital representation highlighting some of their favorite things. They had such pride in creating something that shared what was best about them! I believe that #REALyouSnaps is a fantastic way for students to celebrate who they are and learn about others!*

How might you use #REALyouSnaps with your students or staff to engage in an authentic strengths (or interests) building activity?

A.B.

J.R.

#BookSnaps Challenge

It has been said that inspiration strikes at the most inconvenient times; some of my best ideas come when I'm either running, driving, or taking a shower—none of which allows me to stop and write any information down.

The #BookSnaps Challenge was one of those shower-inspired ideas. I was reflecting on the long days of May 2017 and the fourteen elementary schools I had been supporting as an instructional coach. The students (and a few of the teachers) had become disengaged as they looked forward to the summer break.

So, while my mind was free to reflect, I began to ask, *How might I encourage teachers and students to keep learning and make the most of these last few weeks before summer break?*

And it hit me: A #BookSnaps challenge!

I had seen teachers occasionally posting students' #BookSnaps on Twitter. Maybe we could do a global challenge in which students all over the world could participate.

The problem was I didn't feel that I had anything for the students to win. What would the grand prize be? After a bit of deliberation, I decided the students could guest blog on my website. It had a few subscribers at that time, and this might encourage students to write for an authentic audience, too.

I came up with one other gift to offer the participants. Each #BookSnaps entry would enter students into a drawing for Google Hangouts with me.

The next day I launched the challenge with a short blog and a YouTube video to explain the details. The results were mind-blowing! Students entered a weekly average of 500 #BookSnaps in the challenge.

Several students asked for a #BookSnaps rubric or some guidelines for winning the challenge. The questions provided the perfect opportunity for me to explain the *why* behind #BookSnaps. Other than including the author and the title of the book, there were no guidelines for creating winning #BookSnaps—nor should there be. I simply wanted the students to enjoy reading and connecting with the text in a way that was meaningful to them. All they had to do was turn that connection into a digital, visual representation of their thinking and share it with the world.

Students collaborated globally with each other using the hashtag. They would ask questions or make comments on the #BookSnaps they saw:

"How did you do that?"

"I love that book, too."

"What app are you using to create your BookSnap?"

They tagged the authors of their books in the #BookSnaps, and several book authors responded back to them. I even had several teachers send me emails and direct messages of how their class had interviewed REAL authors via Google Hangout (GHO) and the meeting was inspired by the #BookSnaps challenge.

Let's not forget the student guest blogs! Precious is an understatement. You can view their posts at tarammartin.com/bereal. The winning bloggers took guest blogging on my website seriously. They were fantastic persuasive writers and encouraged readers to add the book they snapped to their summer reading lists.

Also, the Google Hangouts with the class winners melted my heart to puddles. Here I was doubting that the students would view a GHO with me as a privilege, but boy was I wrong! They were captivated by leading the conversation and having me listen to their ideas and share parts of my story with them.

The #BookSnaps Challenge exceeded all of my expectations, and it was all about students sharing their relatable connections to the text they were reading, exposing vulnerability by sharing their thinking with an authentic audience, approaching authors and students around the globe with curious questions that led them to learn through this experience. #BookSnaps are REAL, heart-healthy salt.

Look for future #BookSnaps Challenges by following my website, tarammartin.com, for more details.

Learning through Life

The #BookSnaps movement seasoned the educational realm in ways I had no idea it might. I give Dave Burgess much gratitude for handing me a much larger salt shaker and helping me sprinkle heart-healthy salt all over the world. As of March 2018, the #BookSnaps strategy is now utilized in sixteen different countries. Students are sharing their learning through digital visual representations in many different content areas. I had no concept this little half-baked idea might have a REAL impact on student learning, but it has, and I am grateful.

The strategy worked because it was relatable and accessible to many students. It advocated for students to express their voice in a non-threatening way, which empowered them to expose vulnerability when explaining their thoughts. Teachers and students opened the doors of their hearts and made themselves approachable. And, of course, we all learned through life—together. I'm thankful I didn't abandon the idea in its beginning stages; it has far exceeded my expectations for connecting students and adults around the world in meaningful learning experiences. And even though my son wasn't too sure about the idea when he first taught me to use Snapchat, he follows my story and occasionally asks about what I'm reading. I'll take that as a win!

When you cannonball in with an idea, you may never know the ripple effect of your splash. Don't hesitate. Jump!

monitor your heart rate

- How might explaining the science behind #BookSnaps help others better understand its effectiveness?
- If you were to create a #BookSnaps cousin, what would it be? Why?
- What current technology tools (or apps) allow learners to create a digital representation of their thinking? Explain how and when you might use them in the school setting.
- What idea will you cannonball in on during the next two weeks? How?

Please share your reflections using the #REALedu hashtag, and visit tarammartin.com/bereal for more Chapter 16 heart-healthy exercises.

#BookSnaps Speak: The Untold Stories

17

As the #BookSnaps movement swept across the nation, and later the world, I received many direct messages on Twitter and a plethora of emails. These personal notes varied in content, but each contained a REAL message that revealed how this heart-healthy salt had begun to season students of all ages and geographic locations.

Messages of Hope

Melisa Hayes, a second-grade teacher in Ohio who is fighting breast cancer, shared with me how #BookSnaps are one of the innovative strategies implemented with her students that kept her stretching to try new things when she was feeling less than stellar. She said she would often go to school in the morning to teach and would leave to take her radiation treatments. Then, "sometimes I would come back after radiation to help the substitute." During these tough times, Melisa engaged her students in #BookSnaps. She said, "#BookSnaps opened the door of creativity and voice! They loved the fact that their books could talk. They were excited to share with one another and outside the classroom walls. They have also begun to find innovative #BookSnaps via app smashing. My kiddos were the best medicine! Them and my family! They made me smile, laugh, dance, and sing throughout diagnosis, surgery, and treatment."

Melisa thanked me for sharing the #BookSnaps strategy with teachers around the world and, through her story, she reminded me that we have no excuse not to provide our students with innovative opportunities. If a teacher can do it while kicking cancer's butt, we can all put forth a little effort and make learning meaningful for our kiddos.

Peeking into the Minds of Students across the World

Many #BookSnaps are shared through the hashtag in multiple languages. In fact, #BookSnaps has become a go-to strategy for students learning a second language. The beauty of the strategy is you don't have to speak the Hebrew, French, etc. to understand them. Through the universal language of images, students express their thinking visibly and allow others to peek into the mind of the reader. It's been encouraging to me to hear from teachers in other parts of the world who are using #BookSnaps to make reading more engaging and memorable for their students.

Adam Hill, a teacher in Hong Kong, said,

#BookSnaps allow my students to express their understanding and appreciation of texts in a way that is relevant and engaging to them. By creating #BookSnaps on current platforms, we can meet our students where they're at in the digital world. My students love to annotate, analyze, and express themselves in this creative

way. For me, #BookSnaps are tremendously valuable as a way of making my students' thinking visible. Saved on Seesaw, their #BookSnaps often spark comments from peers, and further conversations begin. Very powerful!"

Brett Salakas, a teacher in an all-girls school in Australia, said,

I first came across the #BookSnaps concept during the Christmas holidays. The #TLAP PLN shared the concept, and the simplistic nature of the idea made it easy to understand and easy to imagine how to incorporate #BookSnaps into my lessons.

"At school, I had been exposed to focused professional development aimed at increasing our staff's expertise at teaching comprehension. We were trained in several strategies, like helping students identify the main idea of a text, and how to locate 'supportive evidence' from the text that reinforces the understanding of the main idea. I could see how using #Booksnaps would fit into my pedagogical approach to teaching reading.

"#BookSnaps changed the way I teach comprehension.

"Teaching students who were too young to have Snapchat accounts was not an issue. My girls (I teach at an all-girl school) used a variety of workarounds. Some used our class Seesaw account, and others used apps like Paint, Canva or PicCollage. I had some students who made 'old school' cut-and-paste jobs where they typed and printed the text from the page and cut out printed emojis and Bitmojis to create that personal connection to the text—paper #booksnaps."

A Cry for Help

#BookSnaps not only allow you to peek into the mind of the reader, sometimes you can see deep into their heart. One particular email certainly caught me off-guard. It was an ordinary Saturday morning, and I opened my email as I was drinking coffee. The words leapt off the screen and gave me a new appreciation for the #BookSnaps movement.

The email came from an eighth-grade English/language arts teacher on the East Coast. At the onset, she made an emphatic statement that the parties within the email have asked to remain anonymous, but the parents wanted to know if they could contact me. My mind immediately jumped to negative thoughts. *Oh, no! Parents on the East coast are upset about #BookSnaps. This could get interesting.* But I continued reading,

Mrs. Q., the ELA teacher, told me she had assigned her students #BookSnaps during their novel study. She did not mention the novel, and by the time I finished reading, I didn't care to know that minor detail. She had told the students to personally connect to the text and upload their #BookSnaps on the shared Padlet (padlet.com). She suggested they each comment on one another's reflections, and how she would be making comments, as well. In the directions, the students could upload as many or as few as they'd like but each student had to share at least one each week.

By the second week of #BookSnaps, Mrs. Q. noticed that "Sam's" #BookSnaps looked much different from the other students. His visual representations were dark, with the broken heart emoji and the sad Bitmoji. Immediately Mrs. Q. looked deeper to see if the connection made sense contextually; she had not remembered this novel being so dark. Sure enough, contextually, Sam was accurate, but the annotation he added to his #BookSnaps let Mrs. Q. know something was not right.

After class, she wrapped him in a side hug, away from the other students, and asked, "Are you okay?"

Sam replied, "Yes. Why?"

She went on to tell him how she was concerned about him and noticed his #BookSnaps connections seemed emotionally different from his peers. She even showed him the Padlet, so he wouldn't think she was crazy. As he scanned the #BookSnaps of all of his peers, his facial expression revealed he had indeed noticed his images standing out from the others. Finally, she said, "I just want you to know I care about you."

You see, Sam came from a middle-class home, didn't play sports, and was not involved in extracurricular clubs, but he was a respectable, straight-A student. He was considered to be a little shy and somewhat insecure but viewed as a child that never gave anyone any trouble—including his parents.

Mrs. Q. noticed Sam tuck his head down after she said she cared. She knelt down and looked him in the eyes (that were now facing the floor) and said, "Sam, is everything okay? Are you okay?"

That's when Sam broke down crying. He told her, "No, everything is not okay. I don't fit in here. I don't belong. No one even notices me at school. I'm just that kid that smiles in the hallway and makes good grades." He went on to explain how he had a well-laid-out plan to take his own life. She did not spell out these details, but I didn't need them.

Tears streamed down my face as I read her account of comforting Sam and contacting his parents. She told them the whole story and, in response, they got Sam the support he needed.

When Sam's parents asked, "What are #BookSnaps?" Mrs. Q. explained they are a way to use a technology tool that students love to share their learning visually. She told them she had learned of the strategy through one of her professional learning network educator friends on Twitter (me) and explained how she had hoped to give students more voice to share their thinking while reading—rather than everything being a prescribed assignment.

Sam's parents immediately realized how it made sense that Sam might speak through Snapchat because he spent hours on the app. "It seems to be his only connection with other students," they said. After Sam had received the therapeutic help he needed, the parents had asked Mrs. Q. if they could email me.

Heart-melting is an understatement. The subject line of their email was, "#BookSnaps saved our son's life. Thank you." Within the body of the text, Sam's parents thanked me for being intentional to find what students love and use it for learning. This was their only child, and they revealed how they had no idea how lonely he had felt.

Being a mom of an only child, a son as well, I felt every word they poured out across that page. In my reply to the parents, I pointed back to the teacher who cared and had heard their son's silent cry for help. "That is what building relationships and listening to our students is all about. Mrs. Q. saved your boy. She listened to him cry out for help, in his Snapchat language, while connecting it to his learning. She read between the lines, or emojis in this case, and didn't waste a minute. She asked him, 'Are you okay?' Mrs. Q. is the one who deserves this gratitude, but I'm so very thankful your boy is doing well and thriving now."

I've checked on Sam one other time since the initial email, and he is doing well. He is now in ninth grade and has joined an extracurricular robotics club.

I never anticipated the depth and breadth of #BookSnaps. Never did I think they would become a language students could use to cry out for life-saving help.

When we stop prescribing students recipes to regurgitate information and allow them to use a language they love to share their thinking, there is no telling how great of an impact we can make on those we serve. If we want to know what the students are thinking, we must provide opportunities for them to share their REAL thoughts. Sam expressed deep vulnerability, and his teacher proved herself relatable and approachable. And all parties involved learned a lesson that saved a precious life.

A Mute Student Finds Her Voice

(The students, teachers, and locations within the story asked to remain anonymous; their names and locations are disguised to honor this request.)

A high school library media specialist sent another compelling email, which completely caught me by surprise. Mrs. Jole. She had assigned her high school students #BookSnaps and prompted them to share their reflections on a shared Padlet (padlet.com); she also encouraged them to comment on each other's posts.

The ages and grade levels of the students varied as the Padlet was shared with the entire high school. She told me how she had imagined the students might be reluctant to post and comment but wanted to try it out and give them the option to share their reflections via #BookSnaps.

As it turned out, the students were uploading #BookSnaps well into the evening and persuading their peers to read their book. It was incredible.

Then, she noticed something extraordinary. A couple of weeks after she introduced the #BookSnaps assignment, what she saw unfolding before her eyes was downright mysterious, miraculous even. It left her covered in chills.

It was Nia!

Nia was a senior in this rural high school. She had a traumatic event occur in her life as a little girl, and at five years old had become a select mute. While Nia spoke fluently before this event, afterward, she had never again uttered a word. She learned to write, communicate via American Sign Language, and read lips like none other, but no sounds escaped her mouth—ever.

No noise.

No words.

But Nia loved Snapchat. She would snap her friend's silly pictures and caption them with slang words and emojis. Nia did not have very many friends, but the few she had knew she was an exuberant, loving young lady.

While reviewing the Padlet one evening, Mrs. Jole saw students uploading #BookSnaps and watched as Nia commented on her peer's reflections. She was so sarcastic and amusing. Then, Mrs. Jole began to tear up as she read the responses to Nia's comments.

"You're hilarious! I had no idea you were so funny."

"I love your wit. I always thought you didn't really understand us."

"What do you think about this book, Nia?"

Nia would comment back and banter back and forth with her classmates. She would make snide remarks about the main character being a "total noob" and how she would have "punched him in the face if she were the girlfriend."

The conversations went back and forth, and, before long, students were standing at the counter of the library checkout desk asking Mrs. Jole if this title or that were available—many of which had been shared through #BookSnaps on the shared Padlet.

The line from Mrs. Jole's email that captured my heart as I read the email was this: "Tara, thank you for sharing the idea of #BookSnaps. Nia finally found her voice and her peers love her. They finally see her wondrous personality and her humorous character. This outlet has turned her senior year into a year to remember—for all of us."

Listen to the #BookSnaps. Students speak through them.

There is no way I could have ever predicted this distinct impact of the #BookSnaps cannonball. It still blows my mind.

Nia has yet to speak a word audibly, but her voice rang loud and clear amongst her classmates. Nia was able to reveal her REALness to her classmates in a way she had yet to discover until this assignment.

In a few years, Snapchat will likely be old news, but students will be connected to something. They will still need an outlet to share their REAL experiences with their peers. Throughout each of these untold stories, one fact remains evident—if we allow students to share their learning and their thinking in ways relevant to their interests, they just might find their voice.

Some might find their voice for the first time in thirteen years!

monitor your heart rate

- In what ways do you allow the voice of those you serve to be heard?
- How do you integrate the interests of those you serve within the learning setting?
- Describe one encounter where a learner shared their REAL voice with you. How did this impact you as an educator?

Please share your reflections using the #REALedu hashtag, and visit tarammartin.com/bereal for more Chapter 17 heart-healthy exercises.

i'm curious
What about?!
I write because
cat
m
i
à
L
dog
+
creature
Guest post?
OM to the G
I'm not sure
Love
I'm not sure...
It's perfect!
Left
Right

Part 5

It's Getting REAL Up in Here

"My favorite teacher empowered me to believe that I can impact others."

—A.J., eleventh grade, Missouri

Be REAL

In the 1980s, I do not think they used the term "at risk" in the school setting. If they had, I would have slid into that category. I did not realize it then and likely thought all children faced the same situations I did.

Somehow I figured out early on that, rather than focusing on the problems in my life, I had to focus on finding the multipliers, the people who would encourage and challenge me to think in new, positive ways. In second grade it was Mrs. S. reaching out and believing in me. Later in life, it was my eleventh-grade teacher, Mrs. Quinn, who helped me hone my writing skills and told me to chase my dreams. Throughout my adolescent years, I listened to sports coaches who gave me feedback and taught me to perform under pressure. As an adult, I have found a handful of pivotal relationships that have stepped into my life and continued to mold my thinking and remind me of that same principle I stood on as a child: What lies ahead is greater than my current circumstances.

These relationships became anchors of hope. When life was almost more than I could bear, I would think back to one of my multipliers, allow their words to ring in my heart and mind, and keep climbing the rungs of life, one step at a time. Although I often felt terrified about the next obstacle, the intent was clear; I would cannon-ball in when I made it to the top of the life ladder.

What made these influential individuals stand out to me years and years later? It sounds much like the student feedback sprinkled throughout the pages of this book: they were REAL.

Easy enough, right?

They were relatable, exposed vulnerability with me, and allowed me to do the same. They were always approachable; I cannot recall one time I felt as if I were bothering them.

And, although I might not have realized it then, they helped me learn through life. I learned something more meaningful than an academic skill; I learned how to persevere and make waves. I learned not only to jump in the water but emit energetic encouragement to those within my realm of influence. I learned that normalizing my weird is powerful. I learned to embrace my interesting quirks and unique characteristics and highlight the ones within those I serve. I learned that we are a force to be reckoned with when we play to our strengths. I learned that being unique is beautiful, and no matter what critics say, we are capable of reaching our seemingly unattainable goals. I learned that there are times I will need to hold the hand of another and take the first jump alongside them, and there are times to get out of the way and let them make a splash.

I didn't need a program or a label to ensure I was future ready. What I needed was a teacher to utter four little words to reshape my thought patterns. She might have said that to every second grader, but, "I believe in you" was exactly what I needed to hear that year. To be honest, each of the relationships mentioned above significantly impacted my life, and that is how these principles became a REAL roadmap within my mind that continues to guide me along life's journey.

It might seem unfathomable that students (or staff members) will make connections with us as educators that transform their trajectory in life, but they do. I am living proof this theory is a fact.

I found this quote taken from a US Department of Education article practical, yet empowering:

> "All children have the ability to experience emotion, but how they experience it and how they learn to manage it may depend a great deal on the relationship with their primary caregiver(s) and other important adults in their lives . . . . A large body of research shows that a strong social and emotional foundation helps boost children's learning, academic performance and other positive long-term outcomes."

The article goes on to state the impact educators have when they foster healthy relationships with their students in the school setting.

> "Within the safe havens of close relationships, children can learn new and more complex skills, like self-regulation, playing with peers, and empathizing with others. These and other dimensions of social and emotional development prepare children for success in school and set the foundation for health and wellness later in life."

The article emphasizes how "positive long-term outcomes" for both students and adults hinge upon "the relationships with important adults in their lives."

You are that person for the learners you serve.

Your actions are unclogging veins of doubt. Your words are freeing the blood clots of the I-can't-accomplish-my-goals-due-to-my-circumstances mentality. Your heart-to-heart empathy is opening the aortic valve and allowing hope to flow through the lives of the learners you lead.

As an educator, we have many responsibilities, but if we are in educational triage, this is one "bypass surgery to the heart" we must make time to perform. The social and emotional status of our students is real. It isn't to be pushed aside or neglected. When we take our real experiences and use them to help others who might face a similar situation or prevent them from going through the same fire, we begin to fulfill our purpose in this life.

If you're a teacher, you might be a Mrs. S. for a little girl (or boy) out there. Don't give up. These special moments create lifelong impact. Do you want to know what students are thinking behind that smile, those crooked pigtails, that stylish clothing, or that disengaged snarl? Then, we need only ask, but they will not be real with us until we are real with them.

Situate the educational stethoscope. What do you hear?

Yes; it is telling us now is the time to be real.

We can be REAL and teach the learning standards necessary for academic success. It is possible. Be Relatable, Expose vulnerability and allow the students to do the same, show yourself Approachable, and Learn through life with those you serve; it could be life-changing, and, in some cases, life-saving.

Now, place your hand over your heart and hold it there for a few seconds. Do you feel that? As long as it is beating and you have breath in your body, you are capable of being REAL and empowering those you serve to say, "This is the REAL me, and I have a purpose in this thing called life."

What are you waiting for? Go! Season the world with your REAL story and encourage everyone you encounter to do the same.

If REAL is the heartbeat of education, what will you do to keep the life source flowing and invigorate our educational system?

Artificial intelligence cannot replicate it; it is up to us!

monitor your heart rate

- What are your key takeaways from *Be REAL: Educate from the Heart*?
- What REAL principle might you apply in the next two weeks? How might that look, sound, and feel?
- Being REAL is a message of hope. What is your REAL story? How has it shaped you into the person you are today? How might it be used to help others overcome their current circumstances?
- In what ways will you encourage those around you to be REAL?

> Please share your reflections using the #REALedu hashtag, and visit tarammartin.com/bereal for more Chapter 18 heart-healthy exercises.

Notes

Introduction

Dictionary.com, "real," April 21, 2018.

Burgess, Dave. *Teach Like a PIRATE: Increase Student Engagement, Boost Your Creativity, and Transform Your Life as an Educator* (San Diego, California: Dave Burgess Consulting, Inc., 2012).

"Heart Disease Facts," *Centers for Disease Control and Prevention*. April 21, 2018. cdc.gov/heartdisease/facts.htm.

Sfard, Anna. "Metaphors for Learning." *Encyclopedia of Science Education*. April 21, 2018. link.springer.com/referenceworkentry/10.1007/978-94-007-6165-0_123-3#page-1.

Chapter 2

Pierson, Rita. "Every Kid Needs a Champion." TED Talks Education. May 2013. ted.com/talks/rita_pierson_every_kid_needs_a_champion.

Chapter 3

Wiseman, Liz. *Multipliers: How the Best Leaders Make Everyone Smarter* (New York, New York: Harper Collins, 2014).

Schein, Edward H. *Humble Inquiry: The Gentle Art of Asking Instead of Telling* (Oakland, California: Berrett-Koehler Publishers, 2013).

Lipton, Laura and Wellman, Bruce. *Mentoring Matters: A Practical Guide for Learning Focused Relationships* (Miravia LLC, 2003).

Chapter 4

Burgess, Dave. *Teach Like a PIRATE: Increase Student Engagement, Boost Your Creativity, and Transform Your Life as an Educator* (San Diego, California: Dave Burgess Consulting, Inc., 2012).

Couros, George. *The Innovator's Mindset: Empower Learning, Unleash Talent, and Lead a Culture of Creativity* (San Diego, California: Dave Burgess Consulting, Inc., 2015).

Chapter 5

"Pulmonary Hypertension," *Mayo Clinic Online*, April 18, 2018. mayoclinic.org/diseases-conditions/ pulmonary-hypertension/home/ovc-20197480.

"What Is the Cardiorespiratory System?" May 1, 2018. reference.com/science/ cardiorespiratory-system-51e02186252080e1.

Young, James B. "Congenital Heart Disease," *Britannica Online*. April 18, 2018. britannica.com/science/congenital-heart-disease. April 18, 2018.

Zak, Paul J. "The Neuroscience of Trust," *Harvard Business Review*. May 5, 2018. hbr.org/2017/01/ the-neuroscience-of-trust.

Part 2

Brown, Brené. *Braving the Wilderness: The Quest for True Belonging and the Courage to Stand Alone* (New York, New York: Random House, 2017).

Chapter 8

Dweck, Carol. *Mindset: The New Psychology of Success* (New York, New York: Ballantine Books, 2007).

Chapter 13

Sinek, Simon. *Start with Why: How Great Leaders Inspire Everyone to Take Action*. (New York, New York: Penguin Random House, 2011).

Chapter15

Adams, Marilyn Jager. *Beginning to Read: Thinking and Learning About Print* (Cambridge, MA: MIT Press, 1990.)

Burns, PhD, Martha. "The Reading Brain: How Your Brain Helps You Read, and Why It Matters." *Scientific Learning*. December 6, 2017. scilearn.com/blog/the-reading-brain.

"A Model of Reading," *National Institute for Professional Practice*. April 18, 2018. professionalpractice.org/about-us/a_model_of_reading.

"How Reading Works," *UROK Learning Institute*. April 18, 2018. uroklearning.com/how-reading-works.

Morris, R. J. "Left Brain, Right Brain, Whole Brain? An examination into the theory of brain lateralization, learning styles and the implications for education," *PGCE Thesis, Cornwall College St Austell*. April 18, 2018. singsurf.org/brain/rightbrain.html.

Macel, Emily. "Beijing's Modern Movement." *Dance Magazine*. February 2009.

"What the Brain Does When It Reads" *LETRS Module 1, 2nd edition*. April 18, 2018. cdn2.hubspot.net/hubfs/208815/2014-15_SchoolYear/LETRS/169261_Letrs2E_M1_29-38.pdf.

Chapter 18

"Social and Emotional Development Research Background," *US Department of Education*. January 18, 2017. www2.ed.gov/about/inits/ed/earlylearning/talk-read-sing/feelings-research.pdf.

Bring Tara Martin
to Your School or Event

Popular Topics from Tara Martin

- Be REAL. Educate from the Heart–Keynote
- #BookSnaps – Snapchat for Annotation & Digital Visualization
- Pirate-Up REAL Group Discussions
- REAL + Innovators' Compass–*A versatile tool for getting unstuck.*
- The Cannonball-In Theory. Make a Splash.
- REAL Talk Treasures–Precious Gems for Meaningful Conversations
- Want to Peek Into the Minds of Learners? For REAL!
- The Beauty of Blogging–The Power of Professional Reflection
- Find Meaning in Sharing Your Learning Journey

For more, visit:

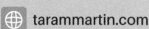 tarammartin.com

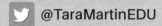 @TaraMartinEDU

#REALedu #BookSnaps

What People Are Saying About Tara Martin

"You are a gem, Tara Martin! You always leave people in a better place than where they were after meeting you."

—Jenny B.

"LOVED @TaraMartinEDU's use of R.E.A.L. + Innovators' Compass in getting to know and support her coaches and how they are turning it around to support their teachers!"

—Ann W.

"My dimple hurts and my brain feels like it's about to explode. Thank you, @TaraMartinEDU."

—Emily G.

"Tara is AMAZING!!! She taught me coaching strategies in 15 minutes to help me on my journey. She empowers ALL those around her and will keep connecting with you! I love that about her!! Thank you, @TaraMartinEDU."

—Nyree

"So amazing meeting @TaraMartinEDU at #CUE18 this morning. She's transforming the game of comprehension with #BookSnaps and making learning fun."

—Missy L.

REAL Thanks

First, I want to thank my God for loving me and reminding me that none of His creations are mistakes. He is my most faithful friend.

I have no doubts, I could not have written this book without my guys, Darrell and Kaleb. They have taught me what being REAL is all about. They are my biggest cheerleaders, and together we stretch each other to chase dreams and crush goals.

To my family and extended family, thank you for the real experiences that have helped mold me into the vessel needed to serve my purpose in this world.

To all students within my realm of influence and beyond, you are the REAL deal, the heartbeat of education.

To all of my fellow educators, mentors, and leaders who have taught me so much along this journey of preparing our future; I appreciate you. We are truly better together.

My PLN—you guys stretch me to cannonball in and grow as an educator every single day. I'm grateful to be connected.

Dave and Shelley Burgess, thank you for taking a chance on me. Your leadership and mentoring are undeniably REAL, and you two mean more to me than words alone can express.

To my astounding book team—Erin Casey, you and your team are outstanding! Thank you for making *Be REAL* real; it has been an honor to work with you all.

Thank you, Jay Billy, for the subtitle suggestion; it is perfect. I appreciate you, mister.

Thank you, Carrie Baughcum, for reading every page of my manuscript and making my words come alive through doodles. Your passion for illustration and visual thinking was precisely what Be REAL needed to become complete. I cannot thank you enough for taking this leap with me; it has been an exciting journey, no doubt.

Interested in more of Carrie's remarkable talent?
Visit Heck Awesome Designs at carriebaughcum.com.

And to all of the little (and big) people in the world—Be REAL; it's enough.

More from

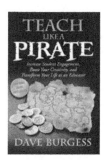

Dave Burgess
Consulting, Inc.

Teach Like a PIRATE

Increase Student Engagement, Boost Your Creativity, and Transform Your Life as an Educator

By Dave Burgess (@BurgessDave)

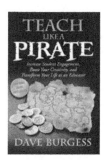

New York Times' bestseller *Teach Like a PIRATE* sparked a worldwide educational revolution with its passionate teaching manifesto and dynamic student-engagement strategies. Translated into multiple languages, it sparks outrageously creative lessons and life-changing student experiences.

Learn Like a PIRATE

Empower Your Students to Collaborate, Lead, and Succeed

By Paul Solarz (@PaulSolarz)

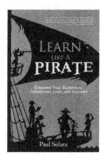

Passing grades don't equip students for life and career responsibilities. *Learn Like a PIRATE* shows how risk-taking and exploring passions in stimulating, motivating, supportive, self-directed classrooms create students capable of making smart, responsible decisions on their own.

P is for PIRATE

Inspirational ABC's for Educators

By Dave and Shelley Burgess (@Burgess_Shelley)

In *P is for Pirate*, husband-and-wife team Dave and Shelley Burgess tap personal experiences of seventy educators to inspire others to create fun and exciting places to learn. It's a wealth of imaginative and creative ideas that make learning and teaching more fulfilling than ever before.

Lead Like a PIRATE

Make School Amazing for Your Students and Staff

By Shelley Burgess and Beth Houf
(@Burgess_Shelley, @BethHouf)

   Lead Like a PIRATE maps out character traits necessary to captain a school or district. You'll learn where to find treasure already in your classrooms and schools—and bring out the best in educators. Find encouragement in your relentless quest to make school amazing for everyone!

Lead with Culture

What Really Matters in Our Schools

By Jay Billy (@JayBilly2)

   In this Lead Like a PIRATE Guide, Jay Billy explains that making school a place where students and staff want to be starts with culture. You'll be inspired by this principal's practical ideas for creating a sense of unity—even in the most diverse communities.

eXPlore Like a Pirate

Gamification and Game-Inspired Course Design to Engage, Enrich, and Elevate Your Learners

By Michael Matera (@MrMatera)

   Create an experiential, collaborative, and creative world with classroom game designer and educator Michael Matera's game-based learning book, *eXPlore Like a Pirate*. Matera helps teachers apply motivational gameplay techniques and enhance curriculum with gamification strategies.

Play Like a Pirate

Engage Students with Toys, Games, and Comics

By Quinn Rollins (@jedikermit)

   In *Play Like a Pirate*, Quinn Rollins offers practical, engaging strategies and resources that make it easy to integrate fun into your curriculum. Regardless of grade level, serious learning can be seriously fun with inspirational ideas that engage students in unforgettable ways.

The Innovator's Mindset

Empower Learning, Unleash Talent, and Lead a Culture of Creativity

By George Couros (@gcouros)

In *The Innovator's Mindset*, teachers and administrators discover that compliance to a scheduled curriculum hinders student innovation, critical thinking, and creativity. To become forward-thinking leaders, students must be empowered to wonder and explore.

Pure Genius

Building a Culture of Innovation and Taking 20% Time to the Next Level

By Don Wettrick (@DonWettrick)

Collaboration—with experts, students, and other educators—helps create interesting and even life-changing opportunities for learning. In *Pure Genius*, Don Wettrick inspires and equips educators with a systematic blueprint for beating classroom boredom and teaching innovation.

Ditch That Textbook

Free Your Teaching and Revolutionize Your Classroom

By Matt Miller (@jmattmiller)

Ditch That Textbook creates a support system, toolbox, and manifesto that can free teachers from outdated textbooks. Miller empowers them to untether themselves, throw out meaningless, pedestrian teaching and learning practices, and evolve and revolutionize their classrooms.

50 Things You Can Do with Google Classroom

By Alice Keeler and Libbi Miller
(@alicekeeler, @MillerLibbi)

50 Things You Can Do with Google Classroom provides a thorough overview of this GAfE app and shortens the teacher learning curve for introducing technology in the classroom. Keeler and Miller's ideas, instruction, and screenshots help teachers go digital with this powerful tool.

50 Things to Go Further with Google Classroom

A Student-Centered Approach

By Alice Keeler and Libbi Miller
(@alicekeeler, @MillerLibbi)

In *50 Things to Go Further with Google Classroom: A Student-Centered Approach*, authors and educators Alice Keeler and Libbi Miller help teachers create a digitally rich, engaging, student-centered environment that taps the power of individualized learning using Google Classroom.

140 Twitter Tips for Educators

Get Connected, Grow Your Professional Learning Network, and Reinvigorate Your Career

By Brad Currie, Billy Krakower, and Scott Rocco
(@bradmcurrie, @wkrakower, @ScottRRocco)

In *140 Twitter Tips for Educators*, #Satchat hosts and founders of Evolving Educators, Brad Currie, Billy Krakower, and Scott Rocco, offer step-by-step instruction on Twitter basics and building an online following within Twitter's vibrant network of educational professionals.

Master the Media

How Teaching Media Literacy Can Save Our Plugged-In World

By Julie Smith (@julnilsmith)

Master the Media explains media history, purpose, and messaging, so teachers and parents can empower students with critical-thinking skills, which lead to informed choices, the ability to differentiate between truth and lies, and discern perception from reality. Media literacy can save the world.

The Zen Teacher

Creating Focus, Simplicity, and Tranquility in the Classroom

By Dan Tricarico (@thezenteacher)

Unrushed and fully focused, teachers influence—even improve—the future when they maximize performance and improve their quality of life. In *The Zen Teacher*, Dan Tricarico offers practical, easy-to-use techniques to develop a non-religious Zen practice and thrive in the classroom.

Your School Rocks . . . So Tell People!

*Passionately Pitch and Promote the Positives Happening
on Your Campus*

By Ryan McLane and Eric Lowe (@McLane_Ryan, @EricLowe21)

Your School Rocks . . . So Tell People! helps schools create effective social media communication strategies that keep students' families and the community connected to what's going on at school, offering more than seventy immediately actionable tips with easy-to-follow instructions and video tutorial links.

The Classroom Chef

*Sharpen Your Lessons. Season Your Classes. Make Math
Meaningful*

By John Stevens and Matt Vaudrey
(@Jstevens009, @MrVaudrey)

With imagination and preparation, every teacher can be *The Classroom Chef* using John Stevens and Matt Vaudrey's secret recipes, ingredients, and tips that help students "get" math. Use ideas as-is, or tweak to create enticing educational meals that engage students.

How Much Water Do We Have?

*5 Success Principles for Conquering Any Challenge and Thriving
in Times of Change*

By Pete Nunweiler with Kris Nunweiler

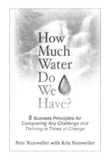

Stressed out, overwhelmed, or uncertain at work or home? It could be figurative dehydration.

How Much Water Do We Have? identifies five key elements necessary for success of any goal, life transition, or challenge. Learn to find, acquire, and use the 5 Waters of Success.

The Writing on the Classroom Wall

*How Posting Your Most Passionate Beliefs about Education Can
Empower Your Students, Propel Your Growth, and Lead to a
Lifetime of Learning*

By Steve Wyborney (@SteveWyborney)

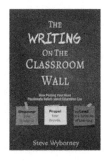

Big ideas lead to deeper learning, but they don't have to be profound to have profound impact. Teacher Steve Wyborney explains why and how sharing ideas sharpens and refines them. It's okay if some ideas fall off the wall; what matters most is sharing and discussing.

Kids Deserve It!

Pushing Boundaries and Challenging Conventional Thinking

By Todd Nesloney and Adam Welcome
(@TechNinjaTodd, @awelcome)

Think big. Make learning fun and meaningful. *Kids Deserve It!* Nesloney and Welcome offer high-tech, high-touch, and highly engaging practices that inspire risk-taking and shake up the status quo on behalf of your students. Rediscover why you became an educator, too!

LAUNCH

Using Design Thinking to Boost Creativity and Bring Out the Maker in Every Student

By John Spencer and A.J. Juliani (@spencerideas, @ajjuliani)

When students identify themselves as makers, inventors, and creators, they discover powerful problem-solving and critical-thinking skills. Their imaginations and creativity will shape our future. John Spencer and A.J. Juliani's *LAUNCH* process dares you to innovate and empower them.

Instant Relevance

Using Today's Experiences to Teach Tomorrow's Lessons

By Denis Sheeran (@MathDenisNJ)

Learning sticks when it's relevant to students. In *Instant Relevance,* author and keynote speaker Denis Sheeran equips you to create engaging lessons *from* experiences and events that matter to students while helping them make meaningful connections between the real world and the classroom.

Escaping the School Leader's Dunk Tank

How to Prevail When Others Want to See You Drown

By Rebecca Coda and Rick Jetter
(@RebeccaCoda, @RickJetter)

Dunk-tank situations—discrimination, bad politics, revenge, or ego-driven coworkers—can make an educator's life miserable. Coda and Jetter (dunk-tank survivors themselves) share real-life stories and insightful research to equip school leaders with tools to survive and, better yet, avoid getting "dunked."

Start. Right. Now.

Teach and Lead for Excellence

By Todd Whitaker, Jeff Zoul, and Jimmy Casas
(@ToddWhitaker, @Jeff_Zoul, @casas_jimmy)

Excellent leaders and teachers *Know the Way, Show the Way, Go the Way, and Grow Each Day*. Whitaker, Zoul, and Casas share four key behaviors of excellence from educators across the U.S. and motivate to put you on the right path.

Teaching Math with Google Apps

50 G Suite Activities

By Alice Keeler and Diana Herrington

(@AliceKeeler, @mathdiana)

Teaching Math with Google Apps meshes the easy student/teacher interaction of Google Apps with G Suite that empowers student creativity and critical thinking. Keeler and Herrington demonstrate fifty ways to bring math classes into the twenty-first century with easy-to-use technology.

Table Talk Math

A Practical Guide for Bringing Math into Everyday Conversations

By John Stevens (@Jstevens009)

In *Table Talk Math*, John Stevens offers parents—and teachers—ideas for initiating authentic, math-based, everyday conversations that get kids to notice and pique their curiosity about the numbers, patterns, and equations in the world around them.

Shift This!

How to Implement Gradual Change for Massive Impact in Your Classroom

By Joy Kirr (@JoyKirr)

Establishing a student-led culture focused on individual responsibility and personalized learning *is* possible, sustainable, and even easy when it happens little by little. In *Shift This!*, Joy Kirr details gradual shifts in thinking, teaching, and approach for massive impact in your classroom.

Unmapped Potential

An Educator's Guide to Lasting Change

By Julie Hasson and Missy Lennard (@PPrincipals)

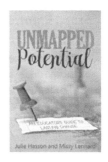

Overwhelmed and overworked? You're not alone, but it can get better. You simply need the right map to guide you from frustrated to fulfilled. *Unmapped Potential* offers advice and practical strategies to forge a unique path to becoming the educator and *person* you want to be.

Shattering the Perfect Teacher Myth

6 Truths That Will Help You THRIVE as an Educator

By Aaron Hogan (@aaron_hogan)

Author and educator Aaron Hogan helps shatter the idyllic "perfect teacher" myth, which erodes self-confidence with unrealistic expectations and sets teachers up for failure. His book equips educators with strategies that help them shift out of survival mode and THRIVE.

Social LEADia

Moving Students from Digital Citizenship to Digital Leadership

By Jennifer Casa-Todd (@JCasaTodd)

A networked society requires students to leverage social media to connect to people, passions, and opportunities to grow and make a difference. *Social LEADia* helps shift focus at school and home from digital citizenship to digital leadership and equip students for the future.

Spark Learning

3 Keys to Embracing the Power of Student Curiosity

By Ramsey Musallam (@ramusallam)

Inspired by his popular TED Talk "3 Rules to Spark Learning," Musallam combines brain science research, proven teaching methods, and his personal story to empower you to improve your students' learning experiences by inspiring inquiry and harnessing its benefits.

Ditch That Homework

Practical Strategies to Help Make Homework Obsolete

By Matt Miller and Alice Keeler (@jmattmiller, @alicekeeler)

In *Ditch That Homework*, Miller and Keeler discuss the pros and cons of homework, why it's assigned, and what life could look like without it. They evaluate research, share parent and teacher insights, then make a convincing case for ditching it for effective and personalized learning methods.

The Four O'Clock Faculty

A Rogue Guide to Revolutionizing Professional Development

By Rich Czyz (@RACzyz)

In *The Four O'Clock Faculty*, Rich identifies ways to make professional learning meaningful, efficient, and, above all, personally relevant. It's a practical guide to revolutionize PD, revealing why some is so awful and what *you* can do to change the model for the betterment of everyone.

Culturize

Every Student. Every Day. Whatever It Takes.

By Jimmy Casas (@casas_jimmy)

Culturize dives into what it takes to cultivate a community of learners who embody innately human traits our world desperately needs—kindness, honesty, and compassion. Casas's stories reveal how "soft skills" can be honed while exceeding academic standards of twenty-first-century learning.

Code Breaker

Increase Creativity, Remix Assessment, and Develop a Class of Coder Ninjas!

By Brian Aspinall (@mraspinall)

You don't have to be a "computer geek" to use coding to turn curriculum expectations into student skills. Use *Code Breaker* to teach students how to identify problems, develop solutions, and use computational thinking to apply and demonstrate learning.

The Wild Card

7 Steps to an Educator's Creative Breakthrough

By Hope and Wade King (@hopekingteach, @wadeking7)

The Kings facilitate a creative breakthrough in the classroom with *The Wild Card*, a step-by-step guide to drawing on your authentic self to deliver your content creatively and be the *wild card* who changes the game for your learners.

Stories from Webb

The Ideas, Passions, and Convictions of a Principal and His School Family

By Todd Nesloney (@TechNinjaTodd)

Stories from Webb goes right to the heart of education. Told by award-winning principal Todd Nesloney and his dedicated team of staff and teachers, this book reminds you why you became an educator. Relatable stories reinvigorate and may inspire you to tell your own!

The Principled Principal

10 Principles for Leading Exceptional Schools

By Jeffrey Zoul and Anthony McConnell
(@Jeff_Zoul, @mcconnellaw)

Zoul and McConnell know from personal experience that the role of a school principal is one of the most challenging *and* the most rewarding in education. Using relatable stories and real-life examples, they reveal ten core values that will empower you to work and lead with excellence.

The Limitless School

Creative Ways to Solve the Culture Puzzle

By Abe Hege and Adam Dovico (@abehege, @adamdovico)

Being intentional about creating a positive culture is imperative for your school's success. This book identifies the nine pillars that support a positive school culture and explains how each stakeholder has a vital role to play in the work of making schools safe, inviting, and dynamic.

Google Apps for Littles

Believe They Can

By Christine Pinto and Alice Keeler
(@PintoBeanz11, @alicekeeler)

Learn how to tap into students' natural curiosity using technology. Pinto and Keeler share a wealth of innovative ways to integrate digital tools in the primary classroom to make learning engaging and relevant for even the youngest of today's twenty-first-century learners.

Be the One for Kids

You Have the Power to Change the Life of a Child

By Ryan Sheehy (@sheehyrw)

Students need guidance to succeed academically, but they also need our help to survive and thrive in today's turbulent world. They need someone to model the attributes that will help them win not just in school but in life as well. That someone is you.

Let Them Speak

How Student Voice Can Transform Your School

By Rebecca Coda and Rick Jetter
(@RebeccaCoda, @RickJetter)

We say, "Student voice matters," but are we really listening? This book will inspire you to find out what your students really think, feel, and need. You'll learn how to listen to and use student feedback to improve your school's culture. All you have to do is ask—and then *Let Them Speak*.

The EduProtocol Field Guide

16 Student-Centered Lesson Frames for Infinite Learning Possibilities

By Marlena Hebren and Jon Corippo
(@mhebern, @jcorippo)

Are you ready to break out of the lesson-and-worksheet rut? Use *The EduProtocol Field Guide* to create engaging and effective instruction, build culture, and deliver content to K–12 students in a supportive, creative environment.

All 4s and 5s

A Guide to Teaching and Leading Advanced Placement Programs

By Andrew Sharos (@AndrewSharosAP)

AP classes shouldn't be relegated to "privileged" schools and students. With proper support, every student can experience success. *All 4s and 5s* offers a wealth of classroom and program strategies that equip you to develop a culture of academic and personal excellence.

Shake Up Learning

Practical Ideas to Move Learning from Static to Dynamic

By Kasey Bell (@ShakeUpLearning)

Is the learning in your classroom static or dynamic? *Shake Up Learning* guides you through the process of creating dynamic learning opportunities—from purposeful planning and maximizing technology to fearless implementation.

The Secret Solution

How One Principal Discovered the Path to Success

Todd Whitaker, Sam Miller, and Ryan Donlan (@ToddWhitaker, @SamMiller29, @RyanDonlan)

An entertaining look at the path to leadership excellence, this parable provides leaders with a non-threatening tool to discuss problematic attitudes in schools. This updated edition includes a reader's guide to help you identify habits and traits that can help you and your team succeed.

The Path to Serendipity

Discover the Gifts along Life's Journey

By Allyson Apsey (@AllysonApsey)

In this funny, genuine, and clever book, Allyson Apsey shares relatable stories and practical strategies for living a meaningful life regardless of the craziness happening around you. You'll discover that you really do have the power to choose the kind of life you live—every day.

The Pepper Effect

Tap into the Magic of Creativity, Collaboration, and Innovation

By Sean Gaillard (@smgaillard)

Using *Sgt. Pepper's Lonely Hearts Club Band* by The Beatles as a template for inspiration, Sean Gaillard explores the necessary steps for creating the conditions for motivation, collaboration, creativity, and innovation in your schoolhouse.

The EduNinja Mindset

11 Habits for Building a Stronger Mind and Body

By Jennifer Burdis (@jennifer_burdis)

As a two-time *American Ninja Warrior* contestant, educator, and trainer, Jen Burdis pushes herself to physically and mentally overcome obstacles. In *The EduNinja Mindset*, Burdis shares her strategies to empower teachers, students and families to develop healthy habits.

About the Author

Tara Martin is an enthusiastic educator, speaker, and author who thrives on change and refuses to settle for the status quo. She has served as a classroom teacher, an instructional coach for several years, and now a district administrator who leads the staff and school communities to meet the curriculum and instructional needs of the student body. Tara also mentors and supervises instructional coaches and provides job-embedded professional development for certified and classified staff.

Tara is a passionate educator who speaks at various conferences to invigorate teachers, administrators, and staff members to apply instructional practices that foster creativity, personalize learning and increase student engagement. She is passionate about discovering the neuroscience behind instructional strategies and believes individualizing adult learning will enhance their ability to flourish and empower students to be the key drivers of their education.

Martin is a connected leader who continually strives to grow professionally. She is always seeking unique ways to make learning fun, relevant, and meaningful. In fact, she is the founder of #BookSnaps, the latest reading comprehension strategy that utilizes Snapchat for EDU-awesomeness, and has taken the world by force in less than a year! Currently, schools in twelve different countries have embraced #BookSnaps to increase student engagement and reading comprehension.

Tara is an inspirational speaker and author. She firmly believes machines and artificial intelligence will never replicate an individual's REAL identity—the unique strengths, talents, and life experiences of every human.

Tara's ambition is to lead a culture of innovative change and to motivate others to become the best they can be, all while staying REAL and never reaching a plateau.

Made in the USA
Coppell, TX
25 January 2021